Physical Characteristics of the Scottish Terrier

(from the American Kennel Club breed standard)

Tail: About seven inches long and never cut. It should be set on high and carried erectly, either vertical or with a slight curve forward. Thick at the base, tapering gradually to a point.

Topline: Firm and level.

Body: Moderately short with ribs extending well back into a short, strong loin, deep flanks and very muscular hindquarters. The ribs should be well sprung out from the spine, forming a broad, strong back, then curving down and inward to form a deep body that would be nearly heart-shaped if viewed in cross-section.

Hindquarters: The thighs should be very muscular and powerful for the size of the dog with the stifles well bent and the legs straight from hock to heel. Hocks should be well let down and parallel to each other.

Coat: Broken coat. It is a hard, wiry outer coat with a soft, dense undercoat.

Size, Proportion, Substance: The Scottish Terrier should have a thick body and heavy bone. The principal objective must be symmetry and balance without exaggeration. Height at withers for either sex should be about 10 inches. The length of back from withers to set-on of tail should be approximately 11 inches. Generally, a well-balanced Scottish Terrier dog should weigh from 19 to 22 pounds and a bitch from 18 to 21 pounds.

Color: Black, wheaten or brindle of any color.

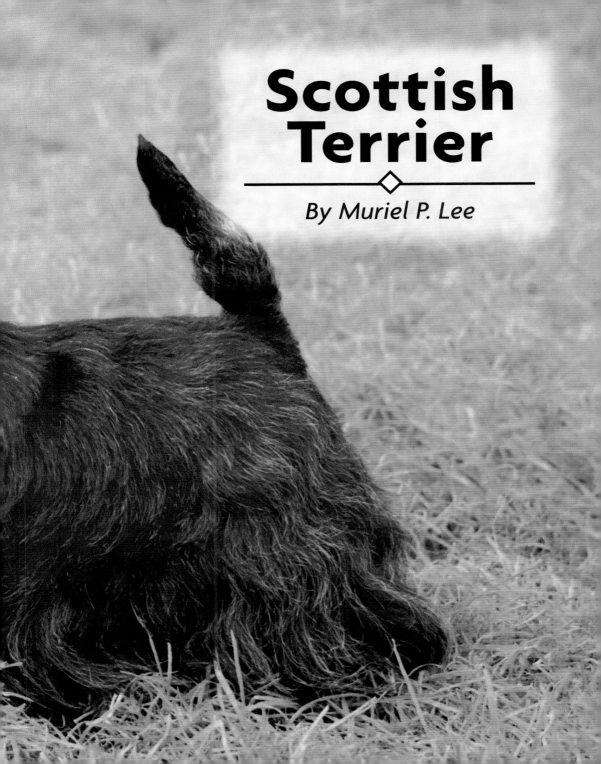

Scottish Terrier

By Muriel P. Lee

Contents

Training Your Scottish Terrier · 78

Begin with the basics of training the puppy and adult dog. Learn the principles of house-training the Scottish Terrier, including the use of crates and basic scent instincts. Enter Puppy Kindergarten and introduce the pup to his collar and leash and progress to the basic commands. Find out about obedience classes and other activities.

Healthcare of Your Scottish Terrier · 102

By Lowell Ackerman DVM, DACVD
Become your dog's healthcare advocate and a well-educated canine keeper. Select a skilled and able veterinarian. Discuss pet insurance, vaccinations and infectious diseases, the neuter/spay decision and a sensible, effective plan for parasite control, including fleas, ticks and worms.

Your Senior Scottish Terrier · 138

Know when to consider your Scottish Terrier a senior and what special needs he will have. Learn to recognize the signs of aging in terms of physical and behavioral traits and what your vet can do to optimize your dog's golden years. Consider some advice about saying goodbye to your beloved pet.

Showing Your Scottish Terrier · 145

Step into the center ring and find out about the world of showing pure-bred dogs. Here's how to get started in AKC shows, how they are organized and what's required for your dog to become a champion. Take a leap into the realms of obedience trials, agility, earthdog events and tracking tests.

KENNEL CLUB BOOKS: SCOTTISH TERRIER
ISBN: 1-59378-257-8

Copyright © 2004
Kennel Club Books, Inc., 308 Main Street, Allenhurst, NJ 07711 USA
Cover Design Patented: US 6,435,559 B2 • Printed in South Korea

Photography by:
Carol Ann Johnson and Alice van Kempen,
with additional photographs by

Paulette Braun, T. J. Calhoun, Carolina Biological Supply, Isabelle Francais, Franklin D. Roosevelt Library, Bill Jonas, Dr. Dennis Kunkel, Tam C. Nguyen, Antonio Philippe and Phototake.

SCOTTISH TERRIER

Sir Paynton Pigott's Granite was the first Scottish Terrier entered in a Kennel Club show. Circa 1877.

The Scottish Terrier is a stalwart dog that hails from the Scottish Highlands. He may be small in size but he is robust, strong of heart and sturdy of limb—truly a big dog in a little package. In the early years, he was called the Aberdeen Terrier after the area from which he came, and the Diehard, due to his staying power when pursuing a fox or other vermin. At first, many may think that the Scottie, with his short, muscular legs and his long head, is out of balance, but once you are used to a Scottie's looks and mannerisms, you will become a lifelong fan of the breed.

This book will give you the history of the breed and tell you about the character of this sturdy dog. You will also learn about puppy care, training and concerns in the breed. From the color photos you will see that this is a smart and attractive dog who makes a wonderful companion. This may not be the breed for everyone, but if you like an active and plucky dog, one that fits easily into city or country life, the Scottie may just be the dog for you.

Perhaps the writer William Haynes said it best: "Words fail me when I want to describe the Scottish Terrier. To me he is the dog of dogs, my personal opinion being all dogs are good; any terrier is better; a Scottie is *best*!...Nobody seems to fall madly in love with a Scottie at first sight, but nobody can live in the same house with him a week and not love him."

THE BEGINNINGS OF THE SCOTTISH TERRIER

In the history of the dog world, the Scottish Terrier is not an old breed; however, its official beginnings, which trace back to the mid-1800s, place it among one of the older breeds recognized by the UK's Kennel Club, which is the registering organization of the Scottie's home country.

The Scottish Terrier belongs to the group of dogs described as terriers, from the Latin word *terra*, meaning "earth." The terrier is a dog that has been bred to work beneath the ground to drive out small and large vermin, rodents and other animals that can be a nuisance to country living.

All of the dogs in the Terrier Group originated in the British Isles with the exception of the Miniature Schnauzer. Many of the terrier breeds were derived from a similar ancestor and, as recently as the mid-1800s, the terriers fell roughly into two basic categories: the rough-coated, short-legged dogs of Scotland and the longer legged, smooth-coated dogs of England.

The family of Scotch Terriers,

The Wire-haired or Scottish Terrier as it looked in 1843.

those bred in Scotland, divide themselves into the modern Scottish Terrier, the West Highland White Terrier, the Cairn Terrier and the Skye Terrier. In the early 1800s, a dog referred to as a Scotch Terrier could be any of the first three breeds mentioned, as inter-breeding was common among these breeds. All three breed types could come from one litter. Often color was the deciding factor in determining the dog's breed.

For many centuries, Scotland had raised a short-legged dog, one that could creep into burrows and cairns and rout out vermin of all shapes and sizes. All of these dogs were derived from the old Scotch Terrier. By 1877, these dogs were shown in the "Hardcoated Scottish Terrier" class, which comprised dogs of questionable lineage that came in a variety of colors. In 1879, The Kennel Club offered classes for

"SCOTCH" TERRIER

Contrary to what many believe, ("Is that a White or a Black Scottie?"), the two dogs on the Scotch bottle are the Scottish Terrier and the West Highland White Terrier. The Scottie has a long muzzle with a longer ear placed high on his head; the Westie has a short, broad muzzle with smaller ears. The Scottish Terrier is a much heavier-boned and heavier-bodied dog than is the Westie.

The attractive white terrier known as the West Highland White Terrier is closely related to the Scottish Terrier. Although the breeds appear quite different today, at one time they could occur in the same litters.

The Cairn Terrier, another handsome short-legged breed from Scotland, is associated with the development of the Scottie.

the Scotch or Broken-haired Terrier, and this marks the official beginning of the Scottish Terrier.

The Scottish Terrier appeared as a distinct breed at The Kennel Club show in London with an entry of 13. The winners were Tartan and the bitch Splinter II. Splinter, when bred to Tartan, produced four champions, of which one was the first great Scottie: Eng. Ch. Dundee.

In 1882, a group of fanciers in Scotland formed a club for the

Scottish Terrier. Although the club disbanded five years later, the group did succeed in drawing up a standard for the breed, a written description of what the ideal Scottish Terrier should look like. This was an early milestone, as now there could be some uniformity in the dogs that were being shown. The standard first published by Vero Shaw in his *Illustrated Book of the Dog* later appeared in 1883 in the Kennel Club Register, where it was titled "Points of the Hard-Haired Scotch Terriers."

In 1883, the Scottish Terrier Club of England was founded with the assistance of Mr. H. J. Ludlow, who was an ardent Scottish Terrier fancier, having bred 8 of the first 20 champions in the breed. Other early dogs who made a significant contribution to the breed were Bonaccord, grandsire of Dundee and Ch. Rascal, who sired only two champions, but another great dog, Seafield, was very closely linebred on Rascal. Seafield was bred to his half-sister and

Bred by Mr. W. Singleton from Ch. Heather Fashion Hint, this is Walsing Wallet, born in 1933 and a champion in 1934.

produced Seafield Rascal in 1898, who was the sire of six champions. Eng. Ch. Alister was the son of Lorna Doone, who was out of Ch. Dundee. If pedigrees could be traced back for enough generations (and if there were a piece of paper large enough!), almost all Scotties would trace their roots back to these dogs. Dorothy Caspersz, in her book *The Popular Scottish Terrier,* traces the old Scottish Terrier lines in depth.

By the 1900s Mr. W. L. McClandish, owner of the famous Ems Kennels, became very active in the breed. Between 1905 and 1912, eight champions were made up in this kennel, in addition to producing the first wheaten champion, Ch. Ems Morning Nip. Mr. McClandish was secretary of the Scottish Terrier Club from 1903 to 1914 and was chairman of The Kennel Club for many years. He was also a writer and his early works on the breed did much to increase

Ch. Gaisgill Monah of Mrs. C. M. Cross's kennels, with two of her puppies who became champions.

Popular Scottish singer Sir Harry Lauder shown with one of his famous Scotties, Ch. Heather Realisation, winner of 11 Challenge Certificates. Sir Harry is dressed in traditional garb for a special occasion.

A. G. Cowley started his breeding program in 1909, managed to keep his kennel going through the war years and stayed very active in the breed through the 1920s and 1930s. He made up 43 British champions, of which 22 were bred by him. Dorothy Caspersz wrote, "Small wonder he was alluded to as the 'Albourne Wizard' and deserved the title. Probably only once in a century is such a being born."

Four dogs referred to as "The Four Horsemen" established the modern type of the Scottish Terrier, and three of these were bred or owned by Cowley. The four dogs were: Eng. Ch. Albourne Barty, Albourne Annie Laurie, Marksman of Docken and Eng. Ch. Heather Necessity. Barty, whelped in 1925, was a black dog, low to the ground and of substantial bone. Barty sired eight champions. In 1928, of the 38 Challenge Certificates awarded by The Kennel Club, Barty's get won 13 of them. Albourne Annie Laurie, considered to be one of the great English producing matrons, produced three champions in one year from a litter sired by Barty. Marksman of Docken was Annie Laurie's littermate, whom Caspersz described as "a great dog in every sense of the word, grandly proportioned throughout...huge bone and powerful quarters...he had terrific charac-

its popularity; some are still used as references on the breed. With the advent of World War I, the Ems Kennel closed, as did many English kennels. There was little breeding and few, if any, dog shows during the war period.

Three breeders came to the fore after World War I: A. G. Cowley of the Albourne Kennels and Robert Chapman Jr. and Sr. of the Heather Kennels. Both of these kennels produced some superior dogs that became standard bearers of the breed on both sides of the Atlantic.

ter and a perfect temperament."
Although he produced no great
sons, his daughters and grand-
daughters proved to be outstanding producers.

The fourth of the "Horse-
men," but certainly not the least,
was the great Heather Necessity
from the Heather Kennels of
Robert Chapman. Robert Chapman and his brother James had a
very successful kennel that domi-
nated the Scottish Terrier scene
in the 1930s. The two brothers
continued the kennel that their
father had started at the turn of
the century. Both brothers had an
eye for a dog, whether it was a
dog they had bred or one they
had purchased. Necessity had
originally been purchased by Mr.
Cowley under the name of
Snookers Double. Entered at a
show at the sale price of £100,
the dog was quickly purchased
by Bob Chapman, who changed
his name to Heather Necessity.
Necessity was used extensively
at stud and was a remarkable
sire. It was generally conceded
that this dog was producing the
stock of a new type that the
breeders were seeking. He had
good length of head, excessive
for those days, a short body, a
rudder for a tail that he carried
erectly, neat little ears and small,
dark eyes of the correct shape.
He sired 10 champion sons, of
which 5 became Best in Show
winners. His son Eng. Ch.

Whelped in 1927, this is Eng. Ch. Heather Necessity, one of the pillars of the breed.

HEATHER NECESSITY'S FIVE BIS SONS:
Eng. Ch. Heather Ambition—Sire of 7 champions
Eng. Ch. Heather Fashion Hint—Sire of 13 English champions, sire of 26 American champions. Sire of Eng. Ch. Heather Realisation
Eng. Ch. Crich Certainty—foundation dog for Deephaven Kennels in the US.
Eng. Ch. Heather Essential—sire of Ch. Hillcote Laddie, sire of 15 American champions
Eng. Ch. Sandheys Silvertip

Heather Fashion Hint, whelped
in 1929, sired 13 champions,
among them the record-breaking
Eng. Ch. Heather
Realisation, whelped in 1934.
Realisation became a champion
at the age of 10 months when he
received his third Challenge
Certificate (CC). He was the
winner of 43 Challenge Certificates, went Best in Show 22
times and was the sire of 6
champions.

A foundation of American bloodlines, Am. Ch. Edgerstoune Troubadour, sired by Walsing Winning Trick of Edgerstoune ex Ch. Edgerstoune Orphan, was himself the sire of 35 champions.

MRS. WINANT AND EDGERSTOUNE

Edgerstoune Kennels, owned by Mrs. John Winant, thrived from the late 1920s until the 1950s. Mrs. Winant imported many fine dogs from England, including the great West Highland White Terrier Ch. Wolvey Pattern of Edgerstoune. John Marvin noted in his book that Mrs. Winant had "an astute ability to pick a winner at home or abroad." Many years ago, she judged a show in England and placed a Westie bitch Best in Show. Immediately after the judging, she bought the bitch and brought her back to America. The acquisition was Ch. Wolvey Pattern of Edgerstoune, who went Best in Show at Westminster. Years later, the same situation was repeated. Again in England, a Mrs. Eppley placed a Scottish Terrier Best in Show and then bought the dog. Ch. Walsing Winning Trick of Edgerstoune emulated Pattern and also reached the pinnacle at Westminster.

The list of great dogs from both the Albourne Kennels and the Heather Kennels is lengthy, and both kennels made a major impact on both sides of the Atlantic. The 1930s have been described as the "golden years" of the Scottish Terrier, and indeed they were, as it is unusual to have two such strong kennels breeding and showing such exceptional stock at the same time.

In addition to Crowley and Chapman, several other individuals should be briefly mentioned. Max Singleton started the Walsing Kennels in the 1930s and became a force in the breed in the 1940s. Dorothy Caspersz was particularly known for her writing ability, and she authored several books on the breed and was a contributor to *Our Dogs* magazine. Dorothy Gabriel also wrote a book on the Scottish Terrier and was a contributor to *Dog World* with her monthly articles on the breed. Both women also judged the breed. Betty Penn-Bull wrote that "Dorothy was a fearless judge and was very forthright and outspoken in her views which were usually full of good sense."

Again, as had happened during World War I, dog breeding more or less came to a standstill in Great Britain with the outbreak of World War II. The first open show held after the war was given by the Scottish Terrier Breeders and Exhibitors' Association in 1945 and drew an entry of 223. In 1946, the first Championship Show was held with an entry of 250 Scotties. It took little time after the war for the Scottie to be on firm footing once again. In 1947, Eng. Ch. Walsing Winning Trick was the first post-war male champion to be made up.

Many kennels became active in the late 1940s; only a few can be mentioned here. Max Singleton, of Walsing, continued to breed and made up about 10 English champions. Walsing Winning Trick, his top dog, was exported to the US, where he won the Best in Show award at the Westminster Kennel Club show, the premier American show. He also sired 23 American champions. Eng. Ch. Wild Winter of Barberry Knowe was also exported to America to the Stalter kennel.

Mr. A. H. James of the Westpark Kennels made up 13 champions. His exceptional dog was Eng. Am. Ch. Westpark Derriford Baffie, winner of 35 CCs, sire of 8 English champions and 20 American champions, and winner of 22 Bests in Show in America. In addition, Eng Ch. Westpark Rio Grande sired 21 American champions and Westpark Masterpiece sired 7 champions.

Miss Betty Penn-Bull of the

Kennelgarth Kennels was a very active breeder and exhibitor who started in the 1930s and continued to exhibit and breed well into the 1980s. Close to 30 English champions have come

OUTSTANDING BARDENE DOGS BRED BY WALTER PALETHORPE:

Eng. Am. Can. Ch. Bardene Boy Blue—imported to US by Anstamm Kennels in 1961. Winner of 7 all-breed Bests in Show, 67 Group firsts. Sired two Scottish Terrier Club of America Lloyd Trophy winners.

Eng. Am. Can. Ch. Bardene Bingo—imported to US by Carnation Kennels in 1964. Top American Terrier in 1966, Best in Show Westminster, Sire of 48 champions, of which 11 became top producers. Sire of Ch. Bardene Bobby Dazzler.

Eng. Am. Can. Ch. Bardene Bobby Dazzler—imported to US by Anstamm Kennels in 1965. Sire of 32 champions, winner of Lloyd Trophy in 1966.

Eng., Am., Can. Ch. Bardene Boy Blue, sire of 41 champions.

out of her kennel, of which the best known was Eng. Ch. Kennelgarth Viking. Viking sired 23 English champions and over 50 champions worldwide. He was the winner of two Bests in Show at major Open Shows. Viking was the sire of Eng. Ch. Gosmore Eilburn Admiration, winner of 22 CCs; Eng. Ch. Gaywyn Viscountess, winner of 15 CCs, and Eng. Ch. Gillsie Highland Lass, dam of

5 champions. Miss Penn-Bull has been a very colorful exhibitor as well as a colorful individual. In 1980 she judged the Scottish Terrier Club of America's national specialty at Montgomery County in Pennsylvania. The author was at that show and was amazed at how her stamina held up through a very large entry and a very wet and cold day.

Mrs. Muriel Owen of the

A well-known Scottish Terrier breeder of the 1930s was Mrs. C. M. Cross. She won acclaim as the owner of kennels which produced some of the finest specimens in the world, examples of which are shown here.

Gaywyn Kennels has been a well-known breeder since the 1940s, and many champions have come out of her kennel. Eng. Ch. Gaywyn Likely Lad, winner of 22 CCs, was exported to the US, where he continued his winning ways. Eng. Ch. Gaywyn Kingson sired 10 champions, and Eng. Ch. Gaywyn Landmark sired 17 champions. Muriel and her husband have hosted many a party during the first week in July, when the English and visiting fanciers have had the opportunity to eat well and socialize at their lovely home. The Gaskells, the Owenses' daughter and her husband, have also produced many champions and winners under the Mayson prefix, particularly Eng. Ch. Mayson Monopoly, who won 32 CCs, sired by Gaywyn Kingson.

Elsie Meyers of the Reanda Kennels was another long-time Scottie breeder and exhibitor. Mrs. Meyers bred at least 30 champions and had some top-winning dogs. Eng. Ch. Reanda Ringold won 20 CCs and Eng. Ch. Reanda Rosita produced 9 champions. Mrs. Meyers continued to breed and exhibit well into the 1980s. Bergit Coady, a very well-known California handler, began her terrier training with Mrs. Meyer.

The Bardene dogs, bred by Walter Palethorpe, have certainly

Eng Ch. Westpark Rio Grande, son of Eng Ch. Westpark Masterpiece, sired 33 champions.

THE OUTSTANDING WESTPARK DOGS:

Westpark Masterpiece—whelped 1945, sired by Walsing Wizard. Sired 7 English champions.

Eng. Ch. Westpark Rio Grande—whelped 1948, sired by Westpark Masterpiece. Sired 12 English champions, 21 American champions. His son Ch. Wyrebury Wrangler sired 21 American champions.

Eng. Am. Ch. Westpark Derriford Baffie—whelped 1952. Grandson of Rio Grande. Sired 7 English champions, 20 American champions. Winner of many Bests in Show, including the Scottish Terrier Club of America's national specialty and Westminster Kennel Club.

influenced the Scottish Terrier in America more than any other kennel in the 1960s and 1970s. Three Bardene dogs were exported to the United States. Eng. Am. Can. Ch. Bardene Bingo was sent to Carnation Kennels, where he was handled by the

Many famous artists, like E. G. Chapman, were intrigued by Scotties and produced many interesting renderings of the breed.

The kennels of Great Britain have not only won and produced well in the UK but their dogs have also continued their winning ways in the ring and in the whelping box in America. The list is too long for this short history, but the following names should be mentioned: Mr. W. Berry of Wyrebury Kennels, Mr. and Mrs. McGill of Glendoune Kennels, Archie MacLaren of Viewpark Kennels and the Gills of Gillsie and Gillson Kennels.

Scottish Terriers were first exported to the United States in the 1880s. By the late 1890s, several exhibitors had become active in showing. In 1902, the

great American terrier handler Bob Bartos. Three consecutive Bests in Show from the classes in both US and Canada finished Bingo's championships. Bingo was the top terrier in 1966 and the winner of the most prestigious American shows.

In 1961, Eng. Am. Can. Ch. Bardene Boy Blue was exported to the kennels of Anthony and Miriam Stamm of Anstamm Kennels. Winner of several Bests in Show, he was also a tremendous producer. In 1965, Eng. Am. Can. Ch. Bardene Bobby Dazzler was also exported to Anstamm and, again, another Bardene dog made his mark in America. These three dogs made a tremendous impact upon the Scottie in the United States.

DOROTHY GABRIEL WROTE ABOUT THE SCOTTIE:

"The character of the Scottish Terrier is wonderful. He is essentially a one man's dog, loving his home and his owner...he is always ready for a long ramble or a day's ratting...He is self-centered, deep natured with a soul both for laughter and tragedy. As a sportsman he is unsurpassed...-Anything that means 'fur' he will kill, from badger to the lowly house mouse, and woe betide the marauding cat that crosses his path, but his own cat is sacred....There is nothing frothy or shallow in the nature of a Scottie...He is absolutely honourable, incapable of a mean or petty action, large hearted and loving, with the soul and mind of an honest gentleman."

The Dutch have always been involved in purebred dogs, the Scottie being no exception. Mrs. Alf Muriel Levison with some of her champion dogs of the 1930s.

first American champion was made up: Ch. Tiree, son of Eng. Ch. Allister. The breed had its ups and downs during the late 1890s until Dr. Fayette Ewing of Louisiana took up the flag and finished two champions in 1900. He worked tirelessly to promote the breed in America. Dr. Ewing bred under the Nosegay prefix and was the first to write an extensive book on the breed. By 1911, the breed had its first Westminster Kennel Club Best in Show winner, Ch. Tickle 'em Jock.

The period from 1920 to 1940 saw startling progress and rise in the Scottish Terrier's popularity. Not only were the British dogs imported but the great British handlers also came to the US with the dogs. In the 1930s, the Scottish Terrier reached the height of its popularity in America, placing third in the American Kennel Club registrations for five years.

During the 1930s, Deephaven Kennels of Ted Bennett in Minneapolis, Minnesota bred 24 champions, with Bob Bartos handling the dogs. Four champion bitches produced a total of 16 champions, and 3 males produced a total of 38 champions. Ch. Deephaven Red Seal was a cornerstone of the breed, producing 25 champions.

Edgerstoune Kennels, owned

Eng. Ch . Greyling of Rookes, owned by Mrs. D. J. Sharp, derived from Heather Ideal. The dog was born in 1932 and achieved the title of champion in 1934.

by Mrs. John Winant, wife of the Ambassador to Great Britain, imported Ch. Walsing Winning Trick, sire of 23 champions and winner of some of the greatest of American shows. Blanche Reeg of Blanart Kennels also bred some top Scots: Ch. Blanart Barcarolle, whelped in 1947, produced 10 champions, and her progeny have produced close to 60 champions. Two of her sons, Ch. Blanart Bolero and Ch. Blanart Barrister, produced a total of 34 champions. Ch. Blanart Bewitching, granddaughter of Barcarolle, won seven all-breed Bests in Show and won the Terrier Group twice at Westminster Kennel Club, in addition to producing seven champions.

Mr. E. H. Stuart of Carnation Kennels, managed by Bob Bartos when Deephaven Kennels closed, bred many champions in addition to importing English dogs. Eng. Ch. Reimill Radiator, son of Westpark Masterpiece, was the sire of 22 champions. Westpark Rio Grande was imported, another top producer in both England and America. Ch. Derriford Baffie also was brought into the kennel. Carnation had the first Best in Show wheaten, Ch. Carnation Golden Girl, in 1951. The great Bardene Bingo was brought over in 1964.

Barberry Knowe Kennels of Mr. and Mrs. Charles Stalter owned and bred a number of top-winning and top-producing Scots. Ch. Barberry Knowe Merrymaker sired 20 champions, Ch. Barberry Knowe Blizzard sired 14 champions, and several other stud dogs sired over 10

STCA TOP HONORS

The Frances G. Lloyd Memorial Trophy, considered to be the Scottish Terrier Club of America's most prestigious award, is presented to the dog or bitch who scores the greatest number of points for Best of Breed based on the championship point rating. It was first presented in 1921, a year after the unexpected death of Mr. Lloyd, who was the founder of Walescott Kennels and a past president of the Scottish Terrier Club of America. It is the only perpetual trophy awarded by the club. The winner's name is engraved on the trophy, which remains in the custody of the STCA and is exhibited at the annual meeting in October. A separate Breeder's Cup Trophy is awarded to the breeder of the Lloyd Trophy.

winners that came out of this kennel was impressive. Ch. Gaidoune Great Bear sired 59 champions and Ch. Gaidoune Tinsel Glow produced 12 champions. Their last Best in Show Scot was Ch. Gaidoune George W. Bear, who represented 7 generations of Gaidoune breeding. By 1976, they had had 20 Best in Show winners in a 20-year period.

John Sheehan of Firebrand Kennels in Minneapolis, Minnesota has a small kennel but over the last 40-plus years he has produced 9 Best in Show dogs. Mr. Sheehan's breeding goes back to the Carnation and Deephaven dogs. His top winner was Am. Can. Ch. Firebrand's Bookmark, sire of 27 champions and winner of 14 Bests in Show. This

champions each. Their top-winning Scot was Ch. Carmichael Fanfare. Handled by Johnny Murphy, she won 32 Bests in Show. She was also the dam of 8 champions. The kennel finished nearly 90 champions.

In the 1950s, Helen Gaither's Gaidoune Kennels in West Virginia was to be one of the last great breeding kennels. The number of champions and

Eng. Ch. Rose Marie of Rookes was bred in 1931.

The Scottish Terrier has been popular in the US for decades, ranking high in annual registrations and often winning top honors at shows. The Scottie has gained a loyal following that few terriers can rival.

The Scots are famous, among other things, for their whiskey, tartans and dogs. Many dog breeds, especially terriers, have originated in Scotland and England.

outstanding dog is behind many of the top-producing dogs in America.

Miriam Stamm, from Anstamm Kennels in Michigan, has been breeding Scots for many years. She originally worked with her husband and, after he passed away, she worked with Cindy Cooke. They imported two of the Bardene dogs and built much of their kennel upon this breeding. They owned the top-producing Scottish Terrier sire of all time in America, Ch. Anstamm Happy Venture, sire of 90 champion get. He sired many top winners and producers. The kennel has won the Scottish Terrier Club of

America's prestigious Lloyd Trophy seven times.

The newer kennels making their mark in America now are Chris and Fred Stephens's Glenby Kennels in Oregon, Debbie Brooks's Deblin Kennels in Maryland and Charla Hill's Charthill Kennels in South Carolina, in addition to many others.

The Scottish Terrier has gained supporters throughout the world. Scotties are seen in the show ring in Canada and Mexico, in South America and South Africa. Sweden has long had a loyal group of breeders, and fanciers in Japan and Italy have been active in the breed for many years. When attending the Montgomery County Kennel Club show in America or the Crufts show in England, fanciers from around the world are at ringside, catalogs in hands and cameras around necks. The Scottie is indeed a well-loved and popular breed!

The grave markers of two cherished pets of President Franklin D. Roosevelt. Fala was a beloved Scottie who lived with him in the White House.

THE FAMOUS FALA

President Franklin D. Roosevelt did much to popularize the Scottish Terrier, as his Scottie Fala was photographed often with him. Much to the dismay of American fanciers, the President preferred his dog "in the rough," and Fala always looked like a "raggedy" Scot! When Fala died, he was buried in Hyde Park, New York, just six feet away from the President. In 1998, a statue of Roosevelt was erected in Washington D.C. with the President in his wheelchair and Fala sitting at his side. When the author was a child, she received a letter from her aunt, who was working in Washington. Her aunt mentioned that when she looked out her office window, she would see a little green bench in the White House garden and often the President's Scottie would be sitting on it.

CHARACTERISTICS OF THE
SCOTTISH TERRIER

The Scottish Terrier is a sturdy dog that projects a masculine, independent and sometimes stubborn attitude. He is a busy dog and likes to be on his toes, watching for squirrels and rabbits, greeting his master and guarding his property. Whatever the job, he is quick and energetic.

The temperament of the Scottie is all terrier. He is quick, alert, intelligent and robust. However, he is a bit less rambunctious than other terrier breeds, and he can have a tendency to be a family or, more particularly, a one-person dog. He likes attention but doesn't want to be overwhelmed. He will sit or lie next to you, but he may not want to sit on your lap. He enjoys a good game or a giggle with his master, but he doesn't

like to be made fun of.

He is sensitive to both praise and blame. He can adjust readily to children, but children must understand his independent nature and his sense of dignity. He will ask little more of you than your love and some conversation. He has a tendency to be rather stubborn, with a mind of his own. He will obey grudgingly and at his own speed. He can quickly figure out what is expected of him and just as quickly work his way around your expectations. He will take patience to train in obedience, but many have achieved success in obedience work. He is a no-nonsense dog. He will not stand in the yard and bark for hours as some dogs will, but if he hears a noise he will alert his owner. He will stand his ground, but his actions are usually defensive, protecting his territory as a sentinel. If pushed into a fight, he will not back down.

As a dog owner, you must be aware of your responsibility toward your friend. You must keep your dog on a leash or in a fenced yard. With the first several sessions of obedience training, you will find that your dog will respond to your commands and will walk beside you as a gentleman. A beginning obedience course will be money and time well spent. You will also have to groom your dog, as this is a breed that requires regular grooming,

ABERDEEN BY CLARA CHEW
For a loving friend in sorrow,
For a frolicsome pal when you're gay,
For a stout and sturdy comrade
Whom storms will not dismay,
Take a bright little dog,
A shaggy little dog,
A little Scottie dog
From Aberdeen.

either by yourself or by a professional groomer.

Second, there are health problems in most breeds, and the Scottish Terrier is no exception; however, the Scottie is considered to be a healthy breed, relatively free from genetic problems. Buy your puppy from a reputable

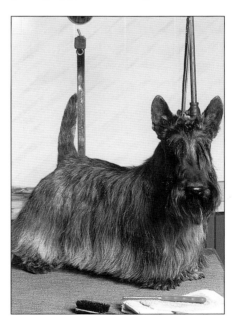

A proper Scottish Terrier requires grooming to look like this! Are you willing to learn how to accomplish this specialized coif?

The Scottie is an active companion, a true go-to-ground terrier in personality, abilities and physical traits.

THE WORKING TERRIER

The purpose of the American Working Terrier Association, founded in 1971, is to encourage and preserve the natural instinct of earth terriers. They are to enter an underground tunnel and react in a positive manner when facing the quarry. A Working Certificate is issued to dogs who qualify for working in a natural den. The AWTA issues Working, Hunting and Gameness Certificates. Scottish Terrier owners enjoy putting their dogs to work and allowing them to use their natural skills, and several Scotties have earned their Certificate of Gameness.

breeder and ask the breeder whether any of the following health problems are in her line.

"Scottie cramp" is an inherited neurological disorder that is seen mainly in the Scottish Terrier. It is carried by a recessive gene and can show up in a pup as early as six to eight weeks. The Scot will be running and playing hard and his rear legs will start to stiffen up or cramp. His body then becomes drawn up and arched; the forelegs stiffen and the dog falls over. In a few seconds, he recovers and is back on his feet. Dogs affected by Scottie cramp can be wonderful pets and their condition can be reduced by giving daily medication. However, dogs who exhibit any degree of Scottie cramp should not be bred.

Von Willebrand's disease (vWD) is the most common bleeding disorder of man and dogs and affects many breeds. This is an inherited disease, and Scotties can be either free of vWD, carriers of the gene or "bleeders." Reputable breeders have their animals' blood tested to make certain that they are not breeding affected dogs.

Epilepsy, seizures, convulsions and "fits" are terms used to describe recurrent seizures caused by a disturbance of brain function. The seizure occurs suddenly and will last about one minute; the dog recovers spontaneously. Sometimes there may be a period of disorientation before complete recovery. The cause of seizures is still being studied; they can be controlled by an anticonvulsant drug that will keep the condition under control.

DELTA SOCIETY

The human/animal bond propels the work of the Delta Society, striving to improve the lives of people and animals. The Pet Partners Program proves that the lives of people and dogs are inextricably linked. The Pet Partners Program, a national registry, trains and screens volunteers for pet therapy in hospices, nursing homes, schools and rehabilitation centers. Dog-and-handler teams of Pet Partners volunteer in all 50 states, with nearly 7,000 teams making visits annually. About 900,000 patients, residents and students receive assistance each year. If you and your dog are interested in becoming Pet Partners, contact the Delta Society online at www.deltasociety.org.

Although black is the most commonly seen color in the Scottie, the wheaten and brindle, shown here, are just as striking.

SCOTTISH TERRIER

A standard is required for every canine breed. The standard will give the breeder and the judge a mental picture of what the specific breed should look like. All reputable breeders strive to produce animals that will meet the standard. Therefore all Scottish Terriers should look like proper Scottish Terriers and, in addition to looking like Scotties, they should have the personality, disposition and intelligence that is sought for in the breed.

The standard is continually studied by serious dog breeders and show judges. However, the reading of the standard is subjective and open to interpretation by the individual who is

The Scottish Terrier is thick-set, powerful and active. The breed's head is characteristically long with a nearly flat skull.

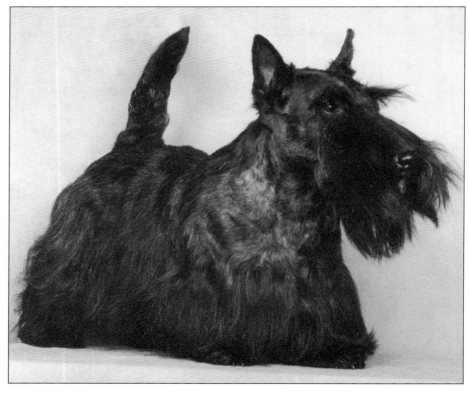

reading it. Standards for any breed are never changed on a whim, and serious study and meetings among breeders take place before any amendments are made.

AMERICAN KENNEL CLUB BREED STANDARD FOR THE SCOTTISH TERRIER

Size, Proportion, Substance: The Scottish Terrier should have a thick body and heavy bone. The principal objective must be symmetry and balance without exaggeration. Height at withers for either sex should be about 10 inches. The length of back from withers to set-on of tail should be approximately 11 inches. Generally, a well-balanced Scottish Terrier dog should weigh from 19 to 22 pounds and a bitch from 18 to 21 pounds.

Head: Long in proportion to the overall length and size of the dog. In profile, the skull and muzzle should give the appearance of two parallel planes.

Skull: Long and of medium width, slightly domed and covered with short, hard hair. In profile, the skull should appear flat. There should be a slight but definite stop between the skull and muzzle at eye level, allowing the eyes to be set in under the brow.

Correct muzzle.   Undesirable muzzle; too short.

Muzzle: Approximately equal to the length of skull with only a slight taper to the nose. A correct Scottish Terrier muzzle should fill an average man's hand.

Nose: Black, regardless of coat color, and of good size, projecting somewhat over the mouth.

Teeth: Large and evenly spaced, having either a scissors or level bite, the former preferred.

Jaw: Square, level and powerful.

Eyes: Set wide apart and well in under the brow. They should be small, bright and piercing, and almond-shaped. The color should be dark brown or nearly black.

Ears: Small, prick, set well up on the skull and pointed, but never cut. From the front, the outer edge of the ear should form a straight line up from the side of the skull.

Correct ears and ear set.

Incorrect ears; set too wide.

Neck: Moderately short, strong, thick and muscular, blending smoothly into well laid back shoulders.

Body: Moderately short with ribs extending well back into a short, strong loin, deep flanks and very muscular hindquarters. The ribs should be well sprung out from the spine, forming a broad, strong back, then curving down and inward to form a deep body that would be nearly heart-shaped if viewed in cross-section.

Topline: Firm and level.

Chest: Broad, very deep and well let down between the forelegs. The forechest should extend well in front of the legs and drop well down into the brisket. The chest should not be flat or concave, and the brisket should nicely fill an average man's slightly-cupped hand.

Tail: About seven inches long and never cut. It should be set on high and carried erectly, either vertical or with a slight curve forward. Thick at the base, tapering gradually to a point.

Forequarters: The shoulders should be well laid back and moderately well knit at the withers. The forelegs should be very heavy in bone, straight or slightly bent with elbows close to the body, and set in under the shoulder blade with a definite forechest in front of them. The forefeet should be larger than the hind feet, round, thick and compact with strong nails. The front feet should point straight ahead, but a slight "toeing out" is acceptable.

Hindquarters: The thighs should be very muscular and powerful for the size of the dog with the stifles well bent and the legs straight from hock to heel. Hocks should be well let down and parallel to each other.

Coat: Broken coat. It is a hard, wiry outer coat with a soft, dense undercoat.

Color: Black, wheaten or brindle of any color.

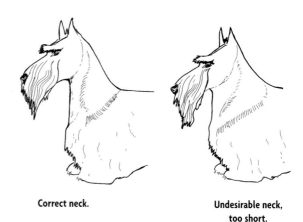

Correct neck.   Undesirable neck, too short.

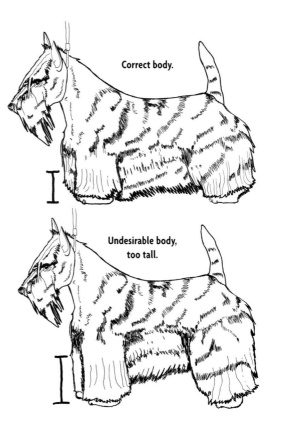

Correct body.

Undesirable body, too tall.

Correct tail.

Incorrect tail.

SCOTTISH TERRIER

WHERE TO BEGIN?

If you are convinced that the Scottish Terrier is the ideal dog for you, it's time to learn about where to find a puppy and what to look for. Locating a litter of Scottish Terriers should not present too much difficulty for the prospective owner. You should inquire about breeders in your area who enjoy a good reputation in the breed. You are looking for an established breeder with outstanding dog ethics and a strong commitment to the breed. New owners should have as many questions as they have doubts. An established breeder is indeed the one to answer your four million questions and make you comfortable with your choice of the Scottish Terrier. An established breeder will sell you a puppy at a fair price if, and only if, the breeder determines that you are a suitable, worthy owner of a Scottie. An established breeder can be relied upon for advice, no matter what time of day or night. A reputable breeder will accept a puppy back, without questions, should you decide that this is not the right dog for you.

When choosing a breeder, reputation is much more important than convenience of location. Do not be overly impressed by breeders who run brag advertisements in the dog publications about their stupendous champions. The real quality breeders are quiet and unassuming. You hear about them at the dog shows and events, by word of mouth. You may be well advised to avoid the novice who lives only a couple of miles away. The local novice breeder, trying so hard to get rid of that first litter of puppies, is more than accommodating and anxious to sell you one. That breeder will charge you as much

TEMPERAMENT ABOVE ALL ELSE

Regardless of breed, a puppy's disposition is perhaps his most important quality. It is, after all, what makes a puppy lovable and "livable." If the puppy's parents or grandparents are known to be snappy or aggressive, the puppy is likely to inherit those tendencies. That can lead to serious problems, such as the dog's becoming a biter, which can lead to eventual abandonment.

as any established breeder. The novice breeder isn't going to interrogate you and your family about your intentions regarding the puppy, the environment and training you can provide, etc. That breeder will be nowhere to be found when your poorly bred, badly adjusted four-pawed monster starts to growl and spit up at midnight or eat the family cat!

Health considerations in the Scottish Terrier are not nearly as daunting as in most other breeds, but responsible, ethical breeders nonetheless take every step to ensure that only the healthiest problem-free stock is used in their matings. Likewise, socialization is a breeder concern of immense importance. Since the Scottish Terrier's temperament can vary from line to line, socialization is the first and best way to encourage a proper, stable personality.

Choosing a breeder is an important first step in dog ownership. Fortunately, the majority of Scottish Terrier breeders is devoted to the breed and its wellbeing. New owners should have little problem finding a reputable breeder in their home state or region. The American Kennel Club and the Scottish Terrier Club of America (STCA) can refer you to breeders of quality Scottish Terriers. STCA members are required to follow a rigid code of

FIRST CAR RIDE
The ride to your home from the breeder will no doubt be your puppy's first automobile experience, and you should make every effort to keep him comfortable and secure. Bring a large towel or small blanket for the puppy to lie on during the trip and an extra towel in case the pup gets carsick or has a potty accident. It's best to have another person with you to hold the puppy in his lap. Most puppies will fall fast asleep from the rolling motion of the car. If the ride is lengthy, your may have to stop so that the puppy can relieve himself, so be sure to bring a leash and collar for those stops. Avoid rest areas for potty trips, since those are frequented by many dogs who may carry parasites or disease. It's better to stop at grassy areas near gas stations or shopping centers to prevent unhealthy exposure for your pup.

SIGNS OF A HEALTHY PUPPY

Healthy puppies are robust little fellows who are alert and active, sporting shiny coats and supple skin. They should not appear lethargic, bloated or pot-bellied, nor should they have flaky skin or runny or crusted eyes or noses. Their stools should be firm and well formed with no evidence of blood or mucus.

Provided you approach the handlers when they are not busy with the dogs, most are more than willing to answer questions, recommend breeders and give advice.

Once you have contacted and met a breeder or two and made your choice about which breeder is best suited to your needs, it's time to visit the litter. Keep in mind that many top breeders have waiting lists. Sometimes new owners have to wait a year or more for a puppy. If you are really committed to the breeder whom you've selected, then you will wait (and hope for an early arrival!). If not, you may have to go with your second- or third-choice breeder. Don't be too anxious, however. If the breeder doesn't have a waiting list, or any customers, there is probably a good reason. It's no different from visiting a restaurant with no clientele. The better establishments always have waiting lists—and it's usually worth the wait. Besides, isn't a puppy more important than a nice meal?

Since you are likely choosing a Scottish Terrier as a pet dog, you simply should select a pup that is friendly and attractive. Scotties are available in three recognized colors, black, wheaten and brindle. Scottish Terriers generally have small litters, averaging four or five puppies, so selection is limited once you

ethics in their breeding programs.

Potential owners are encouraged to attend dog shows to see the Scottish Terriers in action, to meet the owners and handlers firsthand and to get an idea of what Scottish Terriers look like outside a photographer's lens.

have located a desirable litter. If you have aspirations to show, the breeder will advise you about which pup shows the most promise. Beware of the shy or overly aggressive puppy; be especially conscious of the nervous Scottish Terrier pup. Don't let sentiment or emotion trap you into buying the runt of the litter.

The sex of your puppy is largely a matter of personal taste, although there is a common belief among those who work with Scottish Terriers that bitches are quicker to learn and generally more loving and faithful. Males learn more slowly but retain the lesson longer. The difference in size is slight.

Breeders commonly allow visitors to see their litters by around the fifth or sixth week, and puppies leave for their new homes around the tenth week. Breeders who permit their puppies to leave early are more interested in a profit than their puppies' well-being. Puppies need to learn the rules of the trade from their dams, and most dams continue teaching the pups manners and dos and don'ts until the pups leave for new homes. Breeders spend significant amounts of time with the Scottish Terrier toddlers so that they are able to interact with the "other species," i.e. humans. Given the long history that dogs and humans have, bonding

SELECTING FROM THE LITTER
Before you visit a litter of puppies, promise yourself that you won't fall for the first pretty face you see! Decide on your goals for your puppy—show prospect, hunting dog, obedience competitor, family companion—and then look for a puppy who displays the appropriate qualities. In most litters, there is an Alpha pup (the bossy puppy) and occasionally a shy fellow who is less confident, with the rest of the litter falling somewhere in the middle. "Middle-of-the-roaders" are safe bets for most families and novice competitors.

between the two species is natural but must be nurtured. A well-bred, well-socialized Scottish Terrier pup wants nothing

Take some time getting to know each pup in the litter and don't be surprised if the right pup picks you!

Are you prepared to add a Scottie pup to your family and provide him with all the comforts of home?

more than to be near you and please you.

Always check the bite of your selected puppy to be sure that it is neither overshot or undershot. This may not be too noticeable on a young puppy, but it is a fairly common problem with certain lines of Scottish Terriers.

MALE OR FEMALE?

Males of most dog breeds tend to be larger than their female counterparts and take longer to mature. Males also can be more dominant and territorial, especially if they are intact. Neutering before one year of age can help minimize those tendencies. Females of most breeds are often less rambunctious and easier to handle. However, individual personalities vary, so the differences are often due to temperament rather than gender.

A COMMITTED NEW OWNER

By now you should understand what makes the Scottish Terrier a most unique and special dog, one that will fit nicely into your family and lifestyle. If you have researched breeders, you should be able to recognize a knowledge-able and responsible Scottish Terrier breeder who cares not only about his pups but also about what kind of owner you will be. If you have completed the final step in your new journey, you have found a litter, or possibly two, of quality Scottish Terrier pups.

A visit with the puppies and their breeder should be an educa-tion in itself. Breed research, breeder selection and puppy visi-tation are very important aspects of finding the puppy of your dreams. Beyond that, these things also lay the foundation for a successful future with your pup. Puppy personalities within each litter vary, from the shy and easy-going puppy to the one who is dominant and assertive, with most pups falling somewhere in between. By spending time with the puppies, you will be able to recognize certain behaviors and what these behaviors indicate about each pup's temperament. Which type of pup will comple-ment your family dynamics is best determined by observing the puppies in action within their "pack." Your breeder's expertise and recommendations are also valuable. Although you may fall in love with a bold and brassy male, the breeder may suggest that another pup would be best for you. The breeder's experience in rearing Scottish Terrier pups and matching their temperaments with appropriate humans offers the best assurance that your pup will meet your needs and expectations. The type of puppy that you select is just as important as your decision that the Scottish Terrier is the breed for you.

The decision to live with a Scottish Terrier is a serious commitment and not one to be taken lightly. This puppy is a living sentient being that will be dependent on you for basic survival for his entire life. Beyond the basics of survival—food, water, shelter and protection—he needs much, much more. The new pup needs love, nurturing and a proper canine education to mold him into a responsible, well-behaved canine citizen. Your Scottish Terrier's health and good manners will need consistent monitoring and regular "tune-ups." So your job as a responsible dog owner will be ongoing throughout every stage of his life. If you are not prepared to accept these responsibilities and commit to them for the next decade, likely longer, then you are not prepared to own a dog of any breed.

Although the responsibilities of owning a dog may at times tax

---

PEDIGREE VS. REGISTRATION CERTIFICATE
Too often new owners are confused between these two important documents. Your puppy's pedigree, essentially a family tree, is a written record of a dog's genealogy of three generations or more. The pedigree will show you the names as well as performance titles of all dogs in your pup's background. Your breeder must provide you with a registration application, with his part properly filled out. You must complete the application and send it to the AKC with the proper fee. Every puppy must come from a litter that has been AKC-registered by the breeder, born in the US and from a sire and dam that are also registered with the American Kennel Club.

The seller must provide you with complete records to identify the puppy. The AKC requires that the seller provide the buyer with the following: breed; sex, color and markings; date of birth; litter number (when available); names and registration numbers of the parents; breeder's name; and date sold or delivered.

---

your patience, the joy of living with your Scottish Terrier far outweighs the workload, and a well-mannered adult dog is worth your time and effort. Before your very eyes, your new Scottie charge will grow up to be your most loyal friend, devoted to you unconditionally.

YOUR SCOTTIE SHOPPING LIST

Just as expectant parents prepare a nursery for their baby, so should you ready your home for the arrival of your Scottish Terrier pup. If you have the necessary puppy supplies purchased and in place before he comes home, it will ease the puppy's transition from the warmth and familiarity of his mom and littermates to the brand-new environment of his new home and human family. You will be too busy to stock up and prepare your house after your pup comes home, that's for sure! Imagine how a pup must feel upon being transported to a strange new place. It's up to you to comfort him and to let your little pup know that he is going to be happy with you!

FOOD AND WATER BOWLS

Your puppy will need separate bowls for his food and water. Stainless steel pans are generally often preferred to plastic bowls since they sterilize better and pups are less inclined to chew on the metal. Heavy-duty ceramic bowls are popular, but consider how often you will have to pick up those heavy bowls! Buy adult-sized pans, as your Scottie puppy will grow into them before you know it.

THE DOG CRATE

If you think that crates are tools of punishment and confinement for when a dog has misbehaved, think again. Most breeders and almost all trainers recommend a crate as the preferred house-training aid as well as for all-around puppy training and safety. Because dogs are natural den creatures that prefer cave-like environments, the benefits of crate use are many. The crate provides the puppy with his very own "safe house," a cozy place to sleep, take a break or seek comfort with a favorite toy; a travel aid to house your dog when on the road, at motels or at the vet's office; a training aid to help teach your puppy proper toileting habits; a place of solitude when non-dog people happen to drop by and don't want a lively puppy—or even a well-behaved adult dog—saying hello or begging for attention.

Crates come in several types, although the wire crate and the

---

WHAT SIZE IS THE RIGHT SIZE?

When purchasing a crate, buy one that will fit an adult-size dog. Puppy crates are poor investments, since puppies quickly outgrow them. The crate should accommodate an adult dog in a standing position, so that he has room to stand up, turn around and lie down comfortably. A larger crate is fine but not necessary for the dog's comfort, as most of his crate time will be spent lying down and napping.

ROCK-A-BYE BEDDING

The wide assortment of dog beds today can make your choice quite difficult, as there are many adorable novelty beds in fun styles and prints. It's wise to wait until your puppy has outgrown the chewing stage before providing him with a dog bed, since he might make confetti out of it. Your puppy will be happy with an old towel or blanket in his crate until he is old enough to resist the temptation to chew up his bed. For a dog of any age, a bed with a washable cover is always a wise choice.

fiberglass airline-type crate are the most popular. Both are safe and your puppy will adjust to either one, so the choice is up to you. The wire crates offer better visibility for the pup as well as better ventilation. Many of the wire crates easily collapse into suitcase-size carriers. The fiberglass crates, similar to those used by the airlines for animal transport, are sturdier and more den-like but do not collapse and are less ventilated than a wire crate, which can be problematic in hot weather. Some of the newer crates are made of heavy plastic mesh; these are very lightweight and fold up into slim-line suitcases. However, a mesh crate might not be suitable for a pup with manic chewing habits.

Don't bother with a puppy-sized crate. Although your Scottish Terrier will be a wee fellow when you bring him home, he will grow up in the blink of an eye and your puppy crate will be useless. Purchase a crate that will accommodate an adult Scottish Terrier. He will stand about 10 inches when full grown, so a medium-sized crate will fit him nicely.

BEDDING AND CRATE PADS

Your puppy will enjoy some type of soft bedding in his "room" (the crate), something he can snuggle into and feel cozy and secure. Old towels or blankets are good choices for a young pup, since he may (and probably will) have a toileting accident or two in the crate or decide to chew on the bedding material. Once he is fully trained and out of the early chewing stage, you can replace the puppy bedding with a permanent crate pad if you prefer. Crate pads and other dog beds run the gamut from inexpensive to high-end doggie-designer styles, but don't splurge on the good stuff until you are sure that your puppy is reliable and won't tear it up or make a mess on it.

PUPPY TOYS

Just as infants and children require objects to stimulate their minds and bodies, puppies need toys to entertain their curious brains, wiggly paws and achy

TOYS 'R SAFE

The vast array of tantalizing puppy toys is staggering. Stroll through any pet shop or pet-supply outlet and you will see that the choices can be overwhelming. However, not all dog toys are safe or sensible. Most very young puppies enjoy soft woolly toys that they can snuggle with and carry around. (You know they have outgrown them when they shred them up!) Avoid toys that have buttons, tabs or other enhancements that can be chewed off and swallowed. Soft toys that squeak are fun, but make sure your puppy does not disembowel the toy and remove (and swallow) the squeaker. Toys that rattle or make noise can excite a puppy, but they present the same danger as the squeaky kind and so require supervision. Hard rubber toys that bounce can also entertain a pup, but make sure the size of the toy is Scottie-appropriate.

teeth. A fun array of safe doggie toys will help satisfy your puppy's chewing instincts and distract him from gnawing on the leg of your antique chair or your new leather sofa. Most puppy toys are cute and look like they would be a lot of fun, but not all are necessarily safe or good for your puppy, so use caution when you go puppy-toy shopping.

Although Scottish Terriers are not known to be voracious chewers like many other dogs, they still love to chew. The best "chewcifiers" are nylon and hard rubber bones, which are safe to gnaw on and come in sizes appropriate for all age groups and breeds. Be especially careful of the softer natural bones, which can splinter or develop dangerous sharp edges; pups can easily swallow or choke on those bone splinters. Veterinarians often tell of surgical nightmares involving bits of splintered bone, because in addition to the danger of choking, the sharp pieces can damage the intestinal tract.

Similarly, rawhide chews, while a favorite of most dogs and puppies, can be equally dangerous. Pieces of rawhide are easily swallowed after they get all gummy from chewing, and dogs have been known to choke on large pieces of ingested rawhide. Rawhide chews should be offered only when you can supervise the puppy.

Soft woolly toys are special puppy favorites. They come in a wide variety of cute shapes and sizes; some look like little stuffed animals. Puppies love to shake them up and toss them about, or simply carry them around. Be careful of fuzzy toys that have button eyes or noses that your pup could chew off and swallow, and make sure that he does not "disembowel" a squeaky toy to remove the squeaker! Braided rope toys are similar in that they are fun to chew and toss around, but they shred easily and the strings are easy to swallow. The strings are not digestible and, if the puppy doesn't pass them in

his stool, he could end up at the vet's office. As with rawhides, your puppy should be closely monitored with rope toys.

If you believe that your pup has ingested one of these forbidden objects, check his stools for the next couple of days to see if he passes them when he defecates. At the same time, also watch for signs of intestinal distress. A call to your veterinarian might be in order to get his advice and be on the safe side.

An all-time favorite toy for puppies (young and old!) is the empty gallon milk jug. Hard plastic juice containers—46 ounces or more—are also excellent. Such

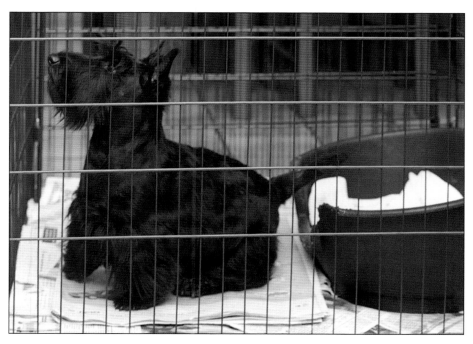

Your Scottie's crate is his own personal space. Wire crates are preferable for Scotties so that they can keep an eye on their surroundings.

EASY, COWBOY!

Who's going to convince your dog that his rawhide toy isn't food? Dogs love rawhide and usually masticate the hide until it's soft enough to swallow. This can lead to choking or intestinal blockage, which is thankfully not terribly common. Another possible danger of rawhide results from the hides used in certain countries. Foreign hides can contain arsenic, lead, antibiotics or *Salmonella*. Even though imported chews are usually cheaper than American-made chews, this is one example in which buying American really counts.

Owners must carefully observe their dogs when they are chewing rawhide and remove any soft pieces that the dog pulls from the hide. Despite these drawbacks, rawhide chews do offer some benefits. Chewing rawhide can help keep the dog's teeth clean and distract your dog from chewing on your favorite leather loafers or sofa.

containers make lots of noise when they are batted about, and puppies go crazy with delight as they play with them. However, they don't often last very long, so be sure to remove and replace them when they get chewed up on the ends.

A word of caution about homemade toys: be careful with your choices of non-traditional play objects. Never use old shoes or socks, since a puppy cannot

distinguish between the old ones on which he's allowed to chew and the new ones in your closet that are strictly off-limits. That principle applies to anything that resembles something that you don't want your puppy to chew up.

COLLARS

A lightweight nylon collar is the best choice for a very young pup. Quick-clip collars are easy to put on and remove, and they can be adjusted as the puppy grows. Introduce him to his collar as soon as he comes home to get him accustomed to wearing it. He'll get used to it quickly and won't mind a bit. Make sure that it is snug enough that it won't slip off, yet loose enough to be comfortable for the pup. You should be able to slip two fingers between the collar and his neck. Check the collar often, as puppies grow in spurts and his collar can become too tight almost overnight. Choke collars are for training purposes only and should never be used on a puppy under four or five months old.

LEASHES

A 6-foot nylon lead is an excellent choice for a young puppy. It is lightweight and not as tempting to chew as a leather lead. You can switch to a 6-foot leather lead after your pup has grown and is used to walking politely on a lead.

KEEP OUT OF REACH

Most dogs don't browse around your medicine cabinet, but accidents do happen! The drug acetaminophen, the active ingredient in Tylenol®, can be deadly to dogs and cats if ingested in large quantities. Acetaminophen toxicity, caused by the dog's swallowing 15 to 20 tablets, can be manifested in abdominal pains within a day or two of ingestion, as well as liver damage. If you suspect your dog has swiped a bottle of Tylenol®, get the dog to the vet immediately so that the vet can induce vomiting and cleanse the dog's stomach.

For initial puppy walks and house-training purposes, you should invest in a shorter lead so that you have more control over the puppy. At first, you don't want him wandering too far away from you, and when taking him out for toileting you will want to keep him in the specific area chosen for his potty spot.

Once the puppy is heel trained with a traditional leash, you can consider purchasing a retractable lead. A flexible lead is excellent for walking adult dogs that are already leash-wise. The "flexi" allows the dog to roam farther away from you and explore a wider area when out walking, and also retracts when you need to keep him close to you.

HOME SAFETY FOR YOUR PUPPY

The importance of puppy-proofing cannot be overstated. In addition to making your house comfortable upon your Scottish Terrier's arrival, you also must make sure that your house is safe for your puppy before you bring him home. There are countless hazards in the owner's personal living environment that a pup can sniff, chew, swallow or destroy. Many are obvious; others are not. Do a thorough advance house check to remove or rearrange those things that could hurt your puppy, keeping any potentially dangerous items out of areas to which he will have access.

Electrical cords are especially dangerous, since puppies view them as irresistible chew toys. Unplug and remove all exposed cords or fasten them beneath a

Two well-trained Scotties out for a stroll with their owner. Notice how nicely the owner is managing two dogs on their retractable leashes.

LEASH LIFE

Dogs love leashes! Believe it or not, most dogs dance for joy every time their owners pick up their leashes. The leash means that the dog is going for a walk—and there are few things more exciting than that! Here are some of the kinds of leashes that are commercially available.

Nylon Leash

Leather Leash

Traditional Leash: Made of cotton, nylon or leather, this is usually about 6 feet in length. A quality-made leather leash is softer on the hands than a nylon one. Durable woven cotton is a popular option. Lengths can vary up to about 48 feet, designed for different uses.

Chain Leash: Usually a metal chain leash with a plastic handle. This is not the best choice for most breeds, as it is heavier than other leashes and difficult to manage.

Retractable Leash: A long nylon cord is housed in a plastic device for extending and retracting. This leash, also known as a flexible leash, is ideal for taking trained dogs for long walks in open areas, although it is not advised for large, powerful breeds. Different lengths and sizes are available, so check that you purchase one appropriate for your dog's weight.

Elastic Leash: A nylon leash with an elastic extension. This is useful for well-trained dogs, especially in conjunction with a head halter. Avoid leashes that are completely elastic, as they afford minimal control to the handler.

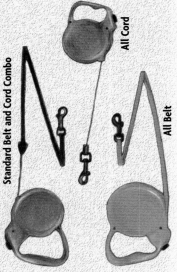

Standard Belt and Cord Combo

All Cord

All Belt

Retractable Leashes

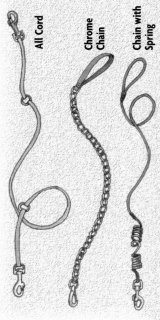

All Cord

Chrome Chain

Chain with Spring

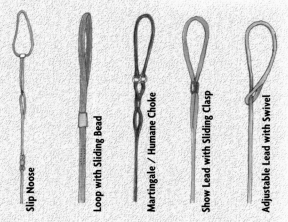

Slip Noose

Loop with Sliding Bead

Martingale / Humane Choke

Show Lead with Sliding Clasp

Adjustable Lead with Swivel

A Variety of Collar-Leash-in-One Products

Adjustable Leash: This has two snaps, one on each end, and several metal rings. It is handy if you need to tether your dog temporarily, but is never to be used with a choke collar.

Tab Leash: A short leash (4 to 6 inches long) that attaches to your dog's collar. This device serves like a handle, in case you have to grab your dog while he's exercising off lead. It's ideal for "half-trained" dogs or dogs that only listen half the time.

Slip Leash: Essentially a leash with a collar built in, similar to what a dog-show handler uses to show a dog. This British-style collar has a ring on the end so that you can form a slip collar. Useful if you have to catch your own runaway dog or a stray.

CONFINEMENT

It is wise to keep your puppy confined to a small "puppy-proofed" area of the house for his first few weeks at home. Gate or block off a space near the door he will use for outdoor potty trips. Expandable baby gates are useful to create puppy's designated area. If he is allowed to roam through the entire house or even several rooms, it will be more difficult to house-train him.

baseboard where the puppy cannot reach them. Veterinarians and firefighters can tell you horror stories about electrical burns and house fires that originated from puppy-chewed electrical cords. Consider this a most serious precaution for your puppy and the rest of your family.

Scout your home for tiny objects that might be seen at a pup's eye level. Keep medication bottles and cleaning supplies well

You only require a lightweight collar and lead for your puppy. A heavier collar and lead will become necessary as the dog matures.

COLLARING OUR CANINES

The standard flat collar with a buckle or a snap, in leather, nylon or cotton, is widely regarded as the everyday all-purpose collar. If the collar fits correctly, you should be able to fit two fingers between the collar and the dog's neck. Such a flat collar is suitable for most breeds of dogs, but greyhound-like dogs (with slender skulls and necks) and thick-necked dogs can easily back out of a collar.

Leather Buckle Collars

The martingale, greyhound or limited-slip collar is preferred by many dog owners and trainers. It is fixed with an extra loop that tightens when pressure is applied to the leash. The martingale collar gets tighter but does not "choke" the dog. The limited-slip collar should only be used for walking and training, not for free play or interaction with another dog. These types of collar should never be left on the dog, as the extra loop can lead to accidents.

Choke collars, usually made of stainless steel, are made for training purposes, though are not recommended for small dogs or heavily coated breeds. The chains can injure small dogs or damage long/abundant coats. Thin nylon choke leads are commonly used on show dogs while in the ring, though these are not practical for everyday use.

Limited-Slip Collar

The harness, with two or three straps that attach over the dog's shoulders and around his torso, is a humane and safe alternative to the conventional collar. By and large, a well-made harness is virtually escape-proof. Harnesses are available in nylon and mesh and can be outfitted on most dogs, ranging from chest girths of 10 to 30 inches.

Harness

Snap Bolt Choke Collar

Nylon Collar

Quick-Click Closure

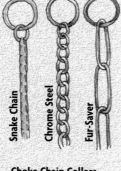

Snake Chain   Chrome Steel   Fur-Saver

Choke Chain Collars

A head collar, composed of a nylon strap that goes around the dog's muzzle and a second strap that wraps around his neck, offers the owner better control over his dog. This device is recommended for problem-solving with dogs (including jumping up, pulling and aggressive behaviors), but must be used with care.

A training halter, including a flat collar and two straps, made of nylon and webbing, is designed for walking. There are several on the market; some are more difficult to put on the dog than others. The halter harness, with two small slip rings at each end, is recommended for ease of use.

PUPPY SHOTS

Puppies are born with natural antibodies that protect them from most canine diseases. They receive more antibodies from the colostrum in their mother's milk. These immunities wear off, however, and must be replaced through a series of vaccines. Puppy shots are given at 3- to 4-week intervals starting at 6 to 8 weeks of age through 12 to 16 weeks of age. Booster shots are given after one year of age, and every one to three years thereafter.

out of reach, and do the same with waste baskets and other trash containers. It goes without saying that you should not use rodent poison or other toxic chemicals in any puppy area, and that you must keep such containers safely locked up. You will be amazed at how many places a curious puppy can discover!

Once your house has cleared inspection, check your yard. A sturdy fence, well embedded into the ground, will give your dog a safe place to play and potty. Although Scottish Terriers are not known to be climbers or fence jumpers, they are still athletic dogs, so a 5- to 6-foot-high fence should be adequate to contain an agile youngster or adult. Check the fence periodically for necessary repairs. If there is a weak link or space to squeeze through, you

can be sure a determined Scottish Terrier will discover it.

The garage and shed can be hazardous places for a pup, as things like fertilizers, chemicals and tools are usually kept there. It's best to keep these areas off-limits to the pup. Antifreeze is especially dangerous to dogs, as they find the taste appealing and it only takes a few licks from the driveway to kill a Scottish Terrier, puppy or adult.

VISITING THE VETERINARIAN
A good veterinarian is your Scottish Terrier puppy's best health insurance policy. If you do not already have a vet, ask friends and experienced dog people in your area for recommendations so that you can select a vet before you bring your Scottish Terrier puppy home. Also arrange for your puppy's first veterinary examination beforehand, since many vets have two- and three-week waiting periods, and your puppy should visit the vet within a day or so of coming home.

It's important to make sure your puppy's first visit to the vet is a pleasant and positive one. The vet should take great care to befriend the pup and handle him gently to make their first meeting a positive experience. The vet will give the pup a thorough physical examination and set up a schedule for vaccinations and other necessary wellness visits. Be sure

A Dog-Safe Home

The dog-safety police are taking you and your new puppy on a house tour. Let's go room by room and see how safe your own home is for your new pup. The following items are doggie dangers, so either they must be removed or the dog should be monitored or not have access to these areas.

Living Room

- house plants (some varieties are poisonous)
- fireplace or wood-burning stove
- paint on the walls (lead-based paint is toxic)
- lead drapery weights (toxic lead)
- lamps and electrical cords
- carpet cleaners or deodorizers

Outdoor

- swimming pool
- pesticides
- toxic plants
- lawn fertilizers

Bathroom

- blue water in the toilet bowl
- medicine cabinet (filled with potentially deadly bottles)
- soap bars, bleach, drain cleaners, etc.
- tampons

Kitchen

- household cleaners in the kitchen cabinets
- glass jars and canisters
- sharp objects (like kitchen knives, scissors and forks)
- garbage can (with remnants of good-smelling things like onions, potato skins, apple or pear cores, peach pits, coffee beans, etc.)

Garage

- antifreeze
- fertilizers (including rose foods)
- pesticides and rodenticides
- pool supplies (chlorine and other chemicals)
- oil and gasoline in containers
- sharp objects, electrical cords and power tools

to show your vet any health and inoculation records, which you should have received from your breeder. Your vet is a great source of canine health information, so be sure to ask questions and take notes. Creating a health journal for your puppy will make a handy reference for his wellness and any future health problems that may arise.

MEETING THE FAMILY

Your Scottish Terrier's homecoming is an exciting time for all members of the family, and it's only natural that everyone will be eager to meet him, pet him and play with him. However, for the puppy's sake, it's best to make these initial family meetings as uneventful as possible so that the pup is not overwhelmed with too much, too soon. Remember, he has just left his dam and his littermates and is away from the breeder's home for the first time. Despite his fuzzy wagging tail, he is still apprehensive and wondering where he is and who all these strange humans are. It's best to let him explore on his own and meet the family members as he feels comfortable. Let him investigate all the new smells, sights and sounds at his own pace. Children should be especially careful to not get overly excited, use loud voices or hug the pup too tightly. Be calm, gentle and affectionate, and be

THE GRASS IS ALWAYS GREENER

Must dog owners decide between their beloved canine pals and their perfectly manicured emerald-green lawns? Just as dog urine is no tonic for growing grass, lawn chemicals are extremely dangerous to your dog. Fertilizers, pesticides and herbicides pose real threats to canines and humans alike. Dogs should be kept off treated grounds for at least 24 hours following treatment. Consider some organic options for your lawn care: use a homemade compost or a natural fertilizer instead of a commercial chemical. Some dog-conscious lawnkeepers avoid fertilizers entirely, keeping up their lawns by watering, aerating, mowing and seeding frequently.

As always, dogs complicate the equation. Canines love grass. They roll in it, eat it and love to bury their noses in it! Grass can mean hours of feel-good, smell-good fun! In addition to the dangers of lawn-care chemicals, there's also the threat of burrs, thorns and pebbles in the grass, not to mention the very common grass allergy. Many dogs develop an incurably itchy skin condition from grass, especially in the late summer.

ready to comfort him if he appears frightened or uneasy.

Be sure to show your puppy his new crate during this first day home. Toss a treat or two inside the crate; if he associates the crate with food, he will associate the crate with good things. If he is comfortable with the crate, you can offer him his first meal inside it. Leave the door ajar so he can wander in and out as he chooses.

FIRST NIGHT IN HIS NEW HOME

So much has happened in your Scottish Terrier puppy's first day away from the breeder. He had his

Breeders monitor the weight gain of each puppy on a daily basis. The breeder should know all about your pup's development and health.

THE FAMILY FELINE

A resident cat has feline squatter's rights. The cat will treat the newcomer (your puppy) as she sees fit, regardless of what you do or say, so it's best to let the two of them work things out on their own terms. Cats have a height advantage and will generally leap to higher ground to avoid direct contact with a rambunctious pup. Some will hiss and boldly swat at a pup who passes by or tries to reach the cat. Keep the puppy under control in the presence of the cat and they will eventually become accustomed to each other.

Here's a hint: move the cat's litter box to where the puppy can't get into it! It's best to do so well before the pup comes home so the cat is used to the new location.

---

first car ride to his new home. He's met his new human family and perhaps the other family pets. He has explored his new house and yard, at least those places where he is to be allowed during his first weeks at home. He may have visited his new veterinarian. He has eaten his first meal or two away from his dam and litter-mates. Surely that's enough to tire out an eight-week-old Scottish Terrier pup...or so you hope!

It's bedtime. During the day, the pup investigated his crate, which is his new den and sleeping space, so it is not entirely strange to him. Line the crate with a soft towel or blanket that he can snuggle into and gently place him in the crate for the night. Some breeders send home a piece of bedding from where the pup slept with his littermates, and those familiar scents are a great comfort for the puppy on his first night without his siblings.

He will probably whine or cry. The puppy is objecting to the confinement and the fact that he is alone for the first time. This can be a stressful time for you as well as for the pup. It's important that you remain strong and don't let the puppy out of his crate to comfort him. He will fall asleep eventually. If you release him, the puppy will learn that crying means "out" and will continue that habit. You are laying the groundwork for future habits. Some breeders find that soft music can soothe a crying pup and help him get to sleep.

SOCIALIZING YOUR PUPPY

The next 20 weeks of your Scottish Terrier puppy's life are the most important of his entire lifetime. A properly socialized puppy will grow up to be a confident and stable adult who will be a pleasure to live with and a welcome addition to the neighborhood.

The importance of socialization cannot be overemphasized. Research on canine behavior has proven that puppies who are not exposed to new sights, sounds, people and animals during their first 20 weeks of life will grow up to be timid and fearful, even aggressive, and unable to flourish outside of their home environment

Socializing your puppy is not difficult and, in fact, will be a fun time for you both. Lead training goes hand in hand with socialization, so your puppy will be learning how to walk on a lead at the same time that he's meeting the neighborhood. Because the Scottish Terrier is a such a terrific breed, your puppy will enjoy being "the new kid on the block." Take him for short walks, to the park and to other dog-friendly places where he will encounter new people, especially children. Puppies automatically recognize children as "little people" and are drawn to play with them. Just

CRATE EXPECTATIONS

To make the crate more inviting to your puppy, you can offer his first meal or two inside the crate, always keeping the crate door open so that he does not feel confined. Keep a favorite toy or two in the crate for him to play with while inside. You can also cover the crate at night with a lightweight sheet to make it more den-like and remove the stimuli of household activity. Never put him in his crate as punishment or as you are scolding him, since he will then associate his crate with negative situations and avoid going there.

SOME DAM ATTITUDE

When selecting a puppy, be certain to meet the dam of the litter. The temperament of the dam is often predictive of the temperament of her puppies. However, dams occasionally are very protective of their young, some to the point of being testy or aggressive with visitors, whom they may view as a danger to their babies. Such attitudes are more common when the pups are very young and still nursing and should not be mistaken for actual aggressive temperament. If possible, visit the dam away from her pups to make friends with her and gain a better understanding of her true personality.

make sure that you supervise these meetings and that the children do not get too rough or encourage him to play too hard. An overzealous pup can often nip too hard, frightening the child and in turn making the puppy overly excited. A bad experience in puppyhood can impact a dog for life, so a pup that has a negative experience with a child may grow up to be shy or even aggressive around children.

Take your puppy along on your daily errands. Puppies are natural "people magnets," and most people who see your pup will want to pet him. All of these encounters will help to mold him into a confident adult dog. Likewise, you will soon feel like a confident, responsible dog owner, rightly proud of your handsome Scottish Terrier.

Be especially careful of your puppy's encounters and experiences during the eight-to-ten-week-old period, which is also called the "fear period." This is a serious imprinting period and all contact during this time should be gentle and positive. A frightening or negative event could leave a permanent impression that could affect his future behavior if a similar situation arises.

Also make sure that your puppy has received his first and second rounds of vaccinations before you expose him to other dogs or bring him to places that other dogs may frequent. Avoid dog parks and other strange-dog areas until your vet assures you that your puppy is fully immunized and resistant to the diseases that can be passed between canines. Discuss socialization with your breeder, as some breeders recommend socializing the puppy even before he has received all his inoculations, depending on how outgoing the breed or puppy may be.

LEADER OF THE PUPPY'S PACK
Like other canines, your puppy needs an authority figure, someone he can look up to and regard as the leader of his "pack." His first pack leader was his dam, who taught him to be polite and not chew too hard on her ears or

A treat for a job well done is a helpful motivator in encouraging your Scottie's good behavior.

nip at her muzzle. He learned those same lessons from his littermates. If he played too rough, they cried in pain and stopped the game, which sent an important message to the rowdy puppy.

As puppies play together, they are also struggling to determine who will be the boss. Being pack animals, dogs need someone to be in charge. If a litter of puppies remained together beyond puppyhood, one of the pups would emerge as the strongest one, the one who calls the shots.

Once your puppy leaves the pack, he will look intuitively for a new leader. If he does not recognize you as that leader, he will try to assume that position for himself. Of course, it is hard to imagine your adorable Scottish Terrier puppy trying to be in charge when he is so small and seemingly helpless. You must remember that these are natural canine instincts. Do not cave in

> **THE CRITICAL SOCIALIZATION PERIOD**
> Canine research has shown that a puppy's 8th through 16th week is the most critical learning period of his life. This is when the puppy "learns to learn," a time when he needs positive experiences to build confidence and stability. Puppies who are not exposed to different people and situations outside the home during this period can grow up to be fearful and sometimes aggressive. This is also the best time for puppy lessons, since he has not yet acquired any bad habits that could undermine his ability to learn.

Teach your puppy correct behavior from the outset. A young puppy should be attentive to your every word...for a little while.

and allow your pup to get the upper "paw!"

Just as socialization is so important during these first weeks, so too is your puppy's early education. He was born without any bad habits. He does not know what is good or bad behavior. If he does things like nipping and digging, it's because he is having fun and doesn't know that humans consider these things as "bad." It's your job to teach him proper puppy manners, and this is the best time to accomplish that...before he has developed bad habits, since it is much more difficult to "unlearn" or correct unacceptable learned behavior than to teach good behavior from the start.

Make sure that all members of the family understand the impor-

tance of being consistent when training their new puppy. If you tell the puppy to stay off the sofa, and your daughter allows him to cuddle on the couch to watch her favorite television show, your pup will be confused about what he is and is not allowed to do. Have a family conference before your pup comes home so that everyone understands the basic principles of puppy training and the rules you have set forth for the pup, and agrees to follow them.

The old adage "a pound of prevention is worth the proverbial pound of cure" is especially true when it comes to puppies. It is much easier to prevent inappropriate behavior than it is to change it. It's also easier and less stressful for the pup, since it will keep discipline to a minimum and create a more positive learning environment for him. That, in turn, will also be easier on you!

Here are a few commonsense tips to keep your belongings safe and your puppy out of trouble:
- Keep your closet doors closed and your shoes, socks and other apparel off the floor so your puppy can't get at them.
- Keep a secure lid on the trash container or put the trash where your puppy can't dig into it. He can't damage what he can't reach!
- Supervise your puppy at all times to make sure he is not getting into mischief. If he starts

to chew the corner of the rug, you can distract him instantly by tossing a toy for him to fetch. You also will be able to whisk him outside when you notice that he is about to piddle on the carpet. If you can't see your puppy, you can't teach or correct his behavior.

SOLVING PUPPY PROBLEMS

CHEWING AND NIPPING

Nipping at fingers and toes is normal puppy behavior. Chewing is also the way that puppies investigate their surroundings. However, you will have to teach your puppy that chewing anything other than his toys is not acceptable. That won't happen overnight and, at times, puppy teeth will test your patience. However, if you allow nipping and chewing to continue, just think about the damage that a mature Scottish Terrier can do with a full set of adult teeth.

Whenever your puppy nips your hand or fingers, cry out "Ouch!" in a loud voice, which should startle your puppy and stop him from nipping, even if only for a moment. Immediately distract him by offering a small treat or an appropriate toy for him to chew instead (which means having chew toys and puppy treats handy or in your pockets at all times). Praise him when he takes the toy and tell him what a

good fellow he is. Praise is just as, or even more, important to puppy training as discipline.

Puppies also tend to nip at children more often than adults, since they perceive little ones to be more vulnerable and more similar to their littermates. Teach your children appropriate responses to nipping behavior and, if they are unable to handle it themselves, you may have to intervene. Puppy nips can be quite painful, and a child's frightened reaction will only encourage a puppy to nip harder, which is a natural canine response. As with all other puppy situations, interaction between your Scottish Terrier puppy and children should be supervised.

Chewing on objects, not just family members' fingers and ankles, is also normal canine

Your puppy has learned his manners from his dam. A well-behaved dam rears nicely mannered pups.

behavior that can be especially tedious (for the owner, not the pup) during the teething period when the puppy's adult teeth are coming in. At this stage, chewing just plain feels good. Furniture legs and cabinet corners are common puppy favorites. Shoes and other personal items also taste pretty good to a pup.

The best solution is, once again, prevention. If you value something, keep it tucked away and out of reach. You can't hide your dining-room table in a closet, but you can try to deflect the chewing by applying a bitter product made just to deter dogs from chewing. Available in a spray or cream, this substance is vile-tasting, although safe for dogs, and most puppies will avoid the forbidden object after one tiny taste. You also can apply the product to your leather leash if the puppy tries to chew on his lead during leash-training sessions.

Opposite ends of the size spectrum! This young Scottie doesn't look intimidated in the shadow of his Old English Sheepdog companion.

> ### MEET AND MINGLE
> Puppies need to meet people and see the world if they are to grow up confident and unafraid. Take your puppy with you on everyday outings and errands. On-lead walks around the neighborhood and to the park offer the pup good exposure to the goings-on of his new human world. Avoid areas frequented by other dogs until your puppy has had his full round of puppy shots; ask your vet when your pup will be properly protected. Arrange for your puppy to meet new people of all ages every week.

Keep a ready supply of safe chews handy to offer your Scottish Terrier as a distraction when he starts to chew on something that's a "no-no." Remember, at this tender age, he does not yet know what is permitted or forbidden, so you have to be "on call" every minute he's awake and on the prowl.

You may lose a treasure or two during puppy's growing-up period, and the furniture could sustain a nasty nick or two. These can be trying times, so be prepared for those inevitable accidents and comfort yourself in knowing that this too shall pass.

JUMPING UP
Although Scottish Terrier pups are not known to be notorious jumpers, they are still puppies

after all, and puppies jump up...on you, your guests, your counters and your furniture. Just another normal part of growing up, and one you need to meet head-on before it becomes an ingrained habit.

The key to jump correction is consistency. You cannot correct your Scottish Terrier for jumping up on you today, then allow it to happen tomorrow by greeting him with hugs and kisses. As you have learned by now, consistency is critical to all puppy lessons.

For starters, try turning your back as soon as the puppy jumps. Jumping up is a means of gaining your attention and, if the pup can't see your face, he may get discouraged and learn that he loses eye contact with his beloved master when he jumps up.

Leash corrections also work, and most puppies respond well to a leash tug if they jump. Grasp the leash close to the puppy's collar and give a quick tug downward, using the command "Off." Do not use the word "Down," since "Down" is used to teach the puppy to lie down, which is a separate action that he will learn during his education in the basic commands. As soon as the puppy has backed off, tell him to sit and immediately praise him for doing so. This will take many repetitions and won't be accomplished quickly, so don't get discouraged or give up...you must be even more persistent than your puppy.

A second method used for jump correction is the spritzer bottle. Fill a spray bottle with water mixed with a bit of lemon

Scottie puppies are curious and fearless. Be certain to monitor your pup whenever he is outdoors, else he may encounter an unfriendly chicken crossing the road.

juice or vinegar. As soon as puppy jumps, command him "Off" and spritz him with the water mixture. Of course, that means having the spray bottle handy whenever or wherever jumping usually happens.

Yet a third method to discourage jumping is grasping the puppy's paws and holding them gently but firmly until he struggles to get away. Wait a brief moment or two, then release his paws and give him the command to sit. He should eventually learn that jumping gets him into an uncomfortable predicament.

Let your Scottie hand out with other well-mannered dogs. This Labrador Retriever proves to be a good influence on his Scottie pal.

Children are major victims of puppy jumping, since puppies view little people as ready targets for jumping up as well as nipping. If your children (or their friends) are unable to dispense jump corrections, you will have to intervene and handle it for them.

Important to prevention is also knowing what you should *not* do. Never kick your Scottish Terrier (for any reason, not just for jumping) or knock him in the chest with your knee. That maneuver could actually harm your puppy. Vets can tell you stories about puppies who suffered broken bones after being banged about when they jumped up.

Puppy Whining

Puppies often cry and whine, just as infants and little children do. It's their way of telling us that they are lonely or in need of attention. Your puppy will miss his littermates and will feel insecure when he is left alone. You may be out of the house or just in another room, but he will still feel alone. During these times, the puppy's crate should be his personal comfort station, a place all his own where he can feel safe and secure. Once he learns that being alone is okay and not something to be feared, he will settle down without crying or objecting. You might want to leave a radio on while he is crated, as the sound of human voices can be soothing and will give the impression that people are around.

Give your puppy a favorite cuddly toy or chew toy to entertain him whenever he is crated. You will both be happier: the puppy because he is safe in his den, and you because he is quiet, safe and not getting into puppy escapades that can wreak havoc in your house or cause him danger.

To make sure that your puppy will always view his crate as a safe and cozy place, never, ever, use the crate as punishment. That's the best way to turn the crate into a negative place that the pup will want to avoid. Sure, you can use the crate for your own peace of mind if puppy is getting into trouble and needs some "time out." Just don't let him know that! Never scold the pup and immediately place him into the crate. Count to ten, give him a couple of hugs and maybe a treat, then scoot him into his crate.

It's also important not to make a big fuss when he is released from the crate. That will make getting out of the crate more appealing than being in the crate, which is just the opposite of what you are trying to achieve.

"COUNTER SURFING"

What we like to call "counter surfing" is a normal extension of jumping and usually starts to happen as soon as a puppy

realizes that he is big enough to stand on his hind legs and investigate the good stuff on the kitchen counter. Once again, you have to be there to prevent it! As soon as you see your Scottish Terrier even start to raise himself up, startle him with a sharp "No!" or "Aaahh, aaahh!" If he succeeds and manages to get one or both paws on the counter, smack those paws (firmly but gently) and tell him "Off!" As soon as he's back on all four paws, command him to sit and praise him at once.

For surfing prevention, make sure to keep any tempting treats or edibles out of reach, where your Scottish Terrier can't see or smell them. It's the old rule of prevention yet again.

Scotties can be aggressive with one another unless properly introduced and acquainted.

SCOTTISH TERRIER

Adding a Scottish Terrier to your household means adding a new family member who will need your care each and every day. When your Scottish Terrier pup first comes home, you will start a routine with him so that, as he grows up, your dog will have a daily schedule just as you do. The aspects of your dog's daily care will likewise become regular parts of your day, so you'll both have a new schedule. Dogs learn by consistency and they thrive on routine: regular times for meals,

exercise, grooming and potty trips are just as important to your dog as they are to you! Your dog's schedule will depend much on your family's daily routine, but remember, you now have a new member of the family who is part of your day, every day!

FEEDING

Feeding your dog the best diet is based on various factors, including age, activity level, overall condition and size. When you visit the breeder, he will share with you his advice about the proper diet for your dog based on his experience with the breed and the foods with which he has had success. Likewise, your vet will be a helpful source of advice throughout the dog's life and will aid you in planning a diet for optimum health.

FEEDING THE PUPPY

Of course, your pup's very first food will be his dam's milk. There may be special situations in which pups fail to nurse, necessitating that the breeder hand-feed them with a formula, but, for the most part, pups spend the first weeks of life nursing from their

---

VARIETY IS THE SPICE

Although dog-food manufacturers contend that dogs don't like variety in their diets, studies show quite the opposite to be true. Dogs would much rather vary their meals than eat the same old chow day in and day out. Dry kibble is no more exciting for a dog than the same bowl of bran flakes would be for you. Fortunately, there are dozens of varieties available on the market, and your dog will likely show preference for certain flavors over others. A word of warning: don't overdo it or you'll develop a fussy eater who only wants the finest delicacies every night.

dam. The breeder weans the pups by gradually introducing solid foods and decreasing the milk meals. Pups may even start themselves off on the weaning process, albeit inadvertently, if they snatch bites from their mom's food bowl.

By the time the pups are ready for new homes, they are fully weaned and eating a good puppy food. As a new owner, you may be thinking, "Great! The breeder has taken care of the hard part!" Not so fast.

A puppy's first year of life is the time when all, or most, of his growth and development takes place. This is a delicate time, and diet plays a huge role in proper skeletal and muscular formation. Improper diet and exercise habits can lead to damaging problems that will compromise the dog's health and movement for his entire life. That being said, new owners should not worry needlessly. With the myriad types of food formulated specifically for growing pups of different-sized breeds, dog-food manufacturers have taken much of the guesswork out of feeding your puppy well. Since growth-food formulas are designed to provide the nutrition that a growing puppy needs, it is unnecessary and, in fact, can prove harmful to add supplements to the diet. Research has shown that too much of certain vitamin supplementation and minerals

FREE-FEEDING
Many owners opt to feed their dogs the free way. That is, serve dry kibble in a feeder, which is available to the dog all day. Arguably, this is the most convenient method of feeding an adult dog, but it may encourage the dog to become fussy about food or defensive over his bowl. Free feeding is only an option for adult dogs, not puppies.

predispose a dog to skeletal problems. It's by no means a case of "if a little is good, a lot is better!" At every stage of your dog's life, too much or too little in the way of nutrients can be harmful, which is why a manufactured complete food is the easiest way to know that your dog is getting what he needs.

Because of a young pup's small body and accordingly small

digestive system, his daily portion will be divided up into small meals throughout the day. This can mean starting off with three or more meals a day and decreasing the number of meals as the pup matures. Eventually you can feed only one meal a day, although it is generally thought that dividing the day's food into two meals on a morning/evening schedule is healthier for the dog's digestion.

DIET DON'TS

- Got milk? Don't give it to your dog! Dogs cannot tolerate large quantities of cows' milk, as they do not have the enzymes to digest lactose.
- You may have heard of dog owners adding raw eggs to their dogs' food for shiny coat or to make the food more palatable, but consumption of raw eggs too often can cause a deficiency of the vitamin biotin.
- Avoid feeding table scraps, as they will upset the balance of the dog's complete food. Additionally, fatty or highly seasoned foods can cause upset canine stomachs.
- Do not offer raw meat to your dog. Raw meat can contain parasites; it also is high in fat.
- Vitamin A toxicity in dogs can be caused by too much raw liver, especially if the dog already gets enough vitamin A in his balanced diet, which should be the case.
- Bones, like chicken, pork-chop and other soft bones, are not suitable, as they easily splinter.

Regarding the feeding schedule, feeding the pup at the same times and in the same place each day is important, both for housebreaking purposes and for establishing the dog's everyday routine. As for the amount to feed, growing puppies generally need proportionately more food per body weight than their adult counterparts, but a pup should never be allowed to gain excess weight. Dogs of all ages should be kept in proper body condition, but extra weight can strain a pup's developing frame, causing skeletal problems.

Watch your pup's weight as he grows and, if the recommended amounts seem to be too much or too little for your pup, consult the vet about appropriate dietary changes. Keep in mind that treats, although small, can quickly add up throughout the day, contributing unnecessary calories. Treats are fine when used prudently; opt for dog treats specially formulated to be healthy, or nutritious snacks like small pieces of cheese or cooked chicken.

FEEDING THE ADULT DOG

For the adult (meaning physically mature) dog, feeding properly is about maintenance, not growth. Again, correct weight is a concern. Your dog should appear fit and should have an evident "waist." His ribs should not be protruding (a sign of being underweight), but they should be covered by only a slight layer of fat. Under normal circumstances, an adult dog can be maintained fairly easily with a good, nutritionally complete adult-formula food.

Factor treats into your dog's overall daily caloric intake, and avoid offering table scraps. Overweight dogs are more prone to health problems. Research has even shown that obesity takes years off a dog's life. With that in mind, resist the urge to overfeed and over-treat. Don't make unnecessary additions to your dog's diet, whether with tidbits or with extra vitamins and minerals.

The amount of food needed for proper maintenance will vary depending on the individual dog's activity level, but you will be able to tell if the daily portions are keeping him in good shape. With the wide variety of good complete foods available, choosing what to feed is largely a matter of personal preference. Just as with the puppy, the adult dog should have consistency in his mealtimes and feeding place. In addition to a consistent routine, regular mealtimes also allow the owner to see how much his dog is eating. If the dog seems never to be satisfied or, likewise, becomes uninterested in his food, the owner will know right away that something is wrong and can consult the vet.

SWITCHING FOODS

There are certain times in a dog's life when it becomes necessary to switch his food; for example, from puppy to adult food and then from adult to senior-dog food. Additionally, you may decide to feed your pup a different type of food than what he received from the breeder, and there may be "emergency" situations in which you can't find your dog's normal brand and have to offer something else temporarily. Anytime a change is made, for whatever reason, the switch must be done gradually. You don't want to upset the dog's stomach or end up with a picky eater who refuses to eat something new. A tried-and-true approach is, over the course of about a week, to mix a little of the new food in with the old, increasing the proportion of new to old as the days progress. At the end of the week, you'll be feeding his regular portions of the new food, and he will barely notice the change!

DIETS FOR THE AGING DOG

A good rule of thumb is that once a dog has reached 75% of his expected lifespan, he has reached "senior citizen" or geriatric status, so your Scottish Terrier will be considered a senior at 10 years of age. Of course, this varies from breed to breed, with the smallest breeds generally enjoying the longest lives and the largest breeds unfortunately being the shortest lived.

QUENCHING HIS THIRST

Is your dog drinking more than normal and trying to lap up everything in sight? Excessive drinking has so many different causes. Obvious causes for a dog's being thirstier than usual are hot weather and vigorous exercise. However, if your dog is drinking more for no apparent reason, you could have cause for concern. Serious conditions like kidney or liver disease, diabetes and various types of hormonal problems can all be indicated by excessive drinking. If you notice your dog's being excessively thirsty, contact your vet at once. Hopefully there will be a simpler explanation, but the earlier a serious problem is detected, the sooner it can be treated with a better rate of cure.

What does aging have to do with your dog's diet? No, he won't get a discount at the local diner's early-bird special. Yes, he will require some dietary changes to accommodate the changes that come along with increased age. One change is that the older dog's dietary needs become more similar to that of a puppy. Specifically, dogs can metabolize more protein as youngsters and seniors than in the adult-maintenance stage. Discuss with your vet whether you need to switch to a higher protein or senior-formulated food, or if your current adult-dog food contains sufficient nutrition for the senior.

Watching the dog's weight remains essential, even more so in the senior stage. Older dogs are already more vulnerable to illness, and obesity only contributes to his susceptibility to problems. As the older dog becomes less active and thus exercises less, his regular portions may cause him to gain weight. At this point, you may consider decreasing his daily food intake or switching to a reduced-calorie food. As with any changes, you should consult your vet for advice.

DON'T FORGET THE WATER!

For a dog, it's always time for a drink! Regardless of what type of food he eats, there's no debate that he needs plenty of water. Fresh, cold water, in a clean bowl, should be freely available to your dog at all times. There are special circumstances, such as during puppy housebreaking, when you will want to monitor your pup's

Selecting the Right Brushes and Combs

Will a rubber curry make my dog look slicker? Is a rake smaller than a pin brush? Do I choose nylon or natural bristles? Buying a dog brush can make the hairs on your head stand on end! Here's a quick once-over to educate you on the different types of brushes.

Slicker Brush: Fine metal prongs closely set on a curved base. Used to remove dead coat from the undercoat of medium- to long-coated breeds.

Pin Brush: Metal pins, often covered with rubber tips, set on an oval base. Used to remove shedding hair and is gentler than a slicker brush.

Metal Comb: Steel teeth attached to a steel handle; the closeness and size of the teeth vary greatly. A "flea comb" has tiny teeth set very closely together and is used to find fleas in a dog's coat. Combs with wider teeth are used for detangling longer coats.

Rake: Long-toothed comb with a short handle. Used to remove undercoat from heavily coated breeds with dense undercoats.

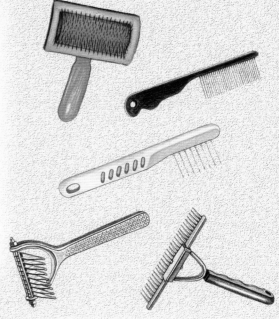

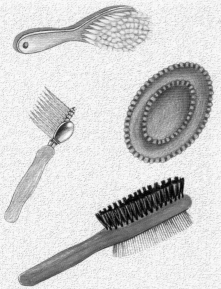

Soft-bristle Brush: Nylon or natural bristles set in a plastic or wood base. Used on short coats or long coats (without undercoats).

Rubber Curry: Rubber prongs, with or without a handle. Used for short-coated dogs. Good for use during shampooing.

Combination Brushes: Two-sided brush with a different type of bristle on each side; for example, pin brush on one side and slicker on the other, or bristle brush on one side and pin brush on the other. An economic choice if you need two kinds of brushes.

Grooming Glove: Sometimes called a hound glove, used to give sleek-coated dogs a once-over.

Make sure your adult Scottie has clean fresh water at all times.

water intake so that you will be able to predict when he will need to relieve himself, but water must be available to him nonetheless. Water is essential for hydration and proper body function just as it is in humans.

You will get to know how much your dog typically drinks in a day. Of course, in the heat or if exercising vigorously, he will be more thirsty and will drink more. However, if he begins to drink noticeably more water for no apparent reason, this could signal any of various problems and you are advised to consult your vet.

Water is the best drink for dogs. Some owners are tempted to give milk from time to time or to moisten dry food with milk, but dogs do not have the enzymes necessary to digest the lactose in milk, which is much different from the milk that nursing puppies receive. Therefore, stick with clean fresh water to quench your dog's thirst, and always have it readily available to him.

GROOMING

BRUSHING

A natural bristle brush or a hound glove can be used for regular routine brushing. Daily brushing is effective for removing dead hair and stimulating the dog's natural oils to add shine and a healthy look to the coat. Although the Scottish Terrier's coat is short and close, it does require a five-minute once-over to keep it looking its shiny best. Regular grooming sessions are also a

THE EARS KNOW

Examining your puppy's ears helps ensure good internal health. The ears are the eyes to the dog's innards! Begin handling your puppy's ears when he's still young so that he doesn't protest every time you lift a flap or touch his ears. Yeast and bacteria are two of the culprits that you can detect by examining the ear. You might notice a strong, often foul, odor, debris, redness or some kind of discharge. All of these point to health problems that can worsen over time. Additionally, you are on the lookout for wax accumulation, ear mites and other tiny bothersome parasites and their even tinier droppings. If your dog has well-furred ears, you may have to pluck hair with tweezers in order to have a better view into the dog's ears, but this is painless if done carefully.

good way to spend time with your dog. Many dogs grow to like the feel of being brushed and will enjoy the daily routine.

The Scottish Terrier is a breed that requires grooming. If you plan to show your dog, you should acquire your Scottish Terrier from a reputable breeder who grooms and shows her dogs. This individual can give you grooming lessons and you can learn how to get your dog ready for the show ring. Grooming is an art that requires time and patience in addition to a good teacher and a student who is willing to take the time to learn. Grooming can be learned from a book but it is difficult.

The Scottie is a double-coated dog. There is a dense, thick undercoat that protects the dog in all kinds of weather and there is a harsh outercoat. Coat care for the pet Scottie can be much different and easier than the coat care for a show dog and if you do not plan to show your dog, you should keep him in a pet trim. The difference between the pet and show coat is that the show dog will have a dense undercoat and on top of it he will have a shiny, harsh coat that will fit him like a jacket. This coat can only be acquired by stripping the body coat with a stripping knife or stripping by hand.

PRESERVING THOSE PEARLY WHITES

What do you treasure more than the smile of your beloved canine pal? Brushing your dog's teeth is just as important as brushing your own. Neglecting your dog's teeth can lead to tooth loss, periodontal disease and inflamed gums, not to mention bad breath. Can you find the time to brush your dog's teeth every day? If not, you should do so once a week at the very least, though every day is truly the ideal. Your vet should give your dog a thorough dental examination during his annual check-ups.

Pet shops sell terrific tooth-care devices, including specially designed toothbrushes, yummy toothpastes and finger-model brushes. You can use a human toothbrush with soft bristles, but never use human toothpastes that can damage the dog's enamel. Baking soda is an option to doggy toothpastes, but your dog will be more receptive to canine toothpastes with the flavor of liver or hamburger. Make tooth care fun for your dog. Let him think that you're "horsing around" with his mouth. When brushing the dog's teeth, begin with the largest teeth (the canines) and proceed back toward the molars.

Within 10 to 12 weeks, and with the proper upkeep, he will have grown from his "underwear" outfit stage into a smart new outfit ready for the ring.

Pet grooming is different from grooming for the show ring, as you use a clipper on the body and scissors for trimming the furnishings and you will have a neat, clean and trimmed dog that will still look like a Scottish Terrier.

Here are the tools that you will need if you are going to do your own grooming:

1. A grooming table, something sturdy with a rubber mat covering the top. You will need a grooming arm, or a "hanger." Your dog will now be comfortable even if confined and you will be able to work on the dog. Grooming is a very difficult and frustrating job if you try to groom without a table and a grooming arm.
2. A metal comb, a slicker brush, a good sharp pair of scissors and a toenail trimmer.
3. Electric clippers with a #10 blade.

To start: Set your dog on the table and put the leash around his neck. Have your leash up behind the ears and have the leash taut when you fasten it to your grooming arm. Take your slicker brush and brush out the entire coat. Brush the whiskers toward the nose, the body hair toward the tail, the tail up toward the tip of the tail. Brush the leg furnishings up toward the body and brush the chest hair down toward the table. Hold the dog up by the front legs and gently brush the stomach hair, first toward the

THE MONTHLY GRIND

If your dog doesn't like the feeling of nail clippers or if you're not comfortable using them, you may wish to try an electric nail grinder. This tool has a small sandpaper disc on the end that rotates to grind the nails down. Some feel that using a grinder reduces the risk of cutting into the quick; this can be true if the tool is used properly. Usually you will be able to tell where the quick is before you get to it. A benefit of the grinder is that it creates a smooth finish on the nails so that there are no ragged edges.

Because the tool makes noise, your dog should be introduced to it before the actual grinding takes place. Turn it on and let your dog hear the noise; turn it off and let him inspect it with you holding it. Use the grinder gently, holding it firmly and progressing a little at a time until you reach the proper length. Look at the nail as you grind so that you do not go too short. Stop at any indication that you are nearing the quick. It will take a few sessions for both you and the puppy to get used to the grinder. A word of caution with long-coated dogs: Do not let his hair get tangled in the grinder!

head and then back toward the rear. For cleanliness, you may want to take your scissors and trim the area around the penis. With the girls, trim some of the hair around the vulva.

Now that your dog is brushed out, comb through the coat with your metal comb. By now you have removed a fair amount of dead hair and your dog will already be looking better. You may find some small mats, and these can be worked out with your fingers or your comb. If you brush your dog out every week or so, you will not have too much of a problem with the mats.

Take your clippers in hand. Your dog will only need to be clipped every three months or so, but you may want to touch up the head more often. Start with the head and follow this pattern: Take your clippers and clip the neck, shoulders and body. Be sure to trim in the direction that the hair lies. Now, take your comb and comb the leg hair down toward the table. Take your scissors and trim the legs neatly.

Take your scissors and trim off anything that "sticks out." If this is your first experience, you may be a bit clumsy, but the hair will grow back in a short time. The finished product may not be quite what you had expected, but expertise will

Regular brushing of your Scottie is absolutely necessary to guarantee a healthy, glossy coat.

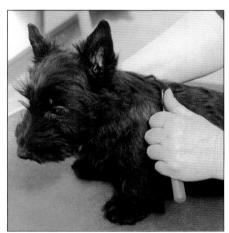

Stripping is required to achieve the desired hard coat of the breed. Introduce the puppy to the stripping knife at any early age.

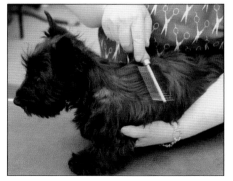

A metal comb is a vital grooming tool in the coat care of your Scottie.

Don't foret to check the teeth. Begin handling your Scottie's mouth from a young age.

come with experience, and you will soon be very proud of your efforts. Your dog should now look like a Scottish Terrier. Put your dog in the sink when you are finished and give him a good bath and rinsing. After toweling him down, return him to the grooming table and trim the toenails on all four legs. At this point you can dry your dog with a blow dryer on a low-heat setting and brush him out again. Or you can let him dry naturally and then brush him out.

If you have grooming problems, you can take your dog to a professional groomer the first time or two for his grooming. The groomer will "set" the pattern and then it will be easier for you to get the Scottie look by following the pattern that is already set in the coat. (Of course, you can eliminate all of the grooming for

yourself, except for the weekly brushing, if you take your dog to the groomer every three months!) If the coat totally grows out before you start to groom, the pattern will be lost and then you will have to start over again. Just remember: many pet owners can trim their dogs as well as professional groomers.

To summarize: your pet should be brushed weekly and bathed as needed. Trim the toenails every month or so and plan to clip the dog every three months. Follow this plan and your dog will be clean, he will have a new "dress" every three months, and he will look like a Scottish Terrier!

BATHING

In general, dogs need to be bathed only a few times a year, possibly more often if your dog gets into something messy or if he starts to smell like a dog. Show dogs are usually bathed before every show, which could be as frequent as weekly, although this depends on the owner. Bathing too frequently can have negative effects on the skin and coat, removing natural oils and causing dryness.

If you give your dog his first bath when he is young, he will become accustomed to the process. Wrestling a dog into the tub or chasing a freshly shampooed dog who has escaped from the bath will be no fun! Most dogs don't naturally enjoy their baths, but you at least want him to cooperate with you.

Before bathing the dog, have the items you'll need close at hand. First, decide where you will bathe the dog. You should have a tub or basin with a non-slip surface. Small dogs can even be bathed in a sink. In warm weather, some like to use a portable pool in the yard, although you'll want to make sure your dog doesn't head for the nearest dirt pile following his bath! You will also need a hose or shower spray to wet the coat thoroughly, a shampoo formulated for dogs, absorbent towels and perhaps a blow dryer. Human shampoos are too harsh for dogs' coats and will dry them out.

Before wetting the dog, give him a brush-through to remove any dead hair, dirt and mats. Make sure he is at ease in the tub and have the water at a comfortable temperature. Begin bathing by wetting the coat all the way down to the skin. Massage in the shampoo, keeping it away from his face and eyes. Rinse him thoroughly, again avoiding the eyes and ears, as you don't want to get water in the ear canals. A thorough rinsing is important, as shampoo residue is drying and itchy to the dog. After rinsing, wrap him in a towel to absorb the initial moisture. You can finish

drying with either a towel or a blow dryer on low heat, held at a safe distance from the dog. You should keep the dog indoors and away from drafts until he is completely dry.

PUPPY LE PEW

On that ill-fated day when your puppy insults the neighborhood skunk by calling him a weasel, you will likely have the unhappy chore of "de-skunking" your dog. Skunks are not afraid of dogs (no less puppies) and will take on an approaching "predator." The skunk's spray is a nasty compound called thiols, a thick, oily liquid that can also be found in decaying flesh or feces. After the skunk hisses, growls and does his "don't-mess-with-me" dance, he sprays the unsuspecting canine.

The age-old remedy was to bathe a "skunked" dog in tomato juice, but thanks to chemist Paul Krebaum, you can put away your can opener. Krebaum provides us with this easy and effective recipe to deodorize your stinky puppy: 1 quart 3% hydrogen peroxide; 1/4 cup baking soda; and 1 teaspoon liquid dish detergent. Work the soapy formula into the dog's coat and keep it out of the dog's eyes. Rinse the dog thoroughly after the bath. Do not make this formula and attempt to bottle it—it will explode! Incidentally, the skunk is in the weasel family, but there's no sense arguing with the nasty-tempered mouse-eating fellow.

Heavy duty nail clippers can be used on adult Scotties.

NAIL CLIPPING

Having his nails trimmed is not on many dogs' lists of favorite things to do. With this in mind, you will need to accustom your puppy to the procedure at a young age so that he will sit still (well, as still as he can) for his pedicures. Long nails can cause the dog's feet to spread, which is not good for him; likewise, long nails can hurt if they unintentionally scratch, not good for you!

Some dogs' nails are worn down naturally by regular walking on hard surfaces, so the frequency with which you clip depends on your individual dog. Look at his nails from time to time and clip as needed; a good way to know when it's time for a trim is if you hear your dog clicking as he walks across the floor.

There are several types of nail clippers and even electric nail-grinding tools made for dogs; first we'll discuss using the clipper. To start, have your clipper ready and some doggie treats on hand. You want your pup to view his nail-clipping sessions in a positive light, and what better way to convince him than with food? You may want to enlist the help of an assistant to comfort the pup and offer treats as you concentrate on the clipping itself. The guillotine-type clipper is thought of by many as the easiest type to use; the nail tip is inserted into the opening and blades on the top and bottom snip it off in one clip.

Start by grasping the pup's paw; a little pressure on the foot pad causes the nail to extend, making it easier to clip. Clip off a little at a time. If you can see the "quick," which is a blood vessel that runs through each nail, you will know how much to trim, as you do not want to cut into the quick. On that note, if you do cut the quick, which will cause bleeding, you can stem the flow of blood with a styptic pencil or other clotting agent. If you mistakenly nip the quick, do not panic or fuss, as this will cause the pup to be afraid. Simply reassure the pup, stop the bleeding and move on to the next nail. Don't be discouraged; you will become a professional canine pedicurist with practice.

You may or may not be able to see the quick, so it's best to just clip off a small bit at a time. If you see a dark dot in the center of the nail, this is the quick and your cue to stop clipping. Tell the puppy he's a "good boy" and offer a piece of treat with each nail. You can also use nail-clipping time to examine the footpads, making sure that they are not dry and cracked and that nothing has become embedded in them.

The nail grinder, the second choice, is many owners' first choice. Accustoming the puppy to the sound of the grinder and sensation of the buzz presents fewer challenges than the clipper, and there's no chance of cutting through the quick. Use the grinder on a low setting and always talk soothingly to your dog. He won't mind his salon visit, and he'll have nicely polished nails as well.

Ear cleaning is a necessary grooming task. Use special ear powder or lotion available from your vet or pet shop.

EAR CLEANING

While keeping your dog's ears clean unfortunately will not cause him to "hear" your commands any better, it will protect him from ear infection and ear-mite infestation. In addition, a dog's ears are vulnerable to waxy build-up and to collecting foreign matter from the outdoors. Look in your dog's ears regularly to ensure that they look pink, clean and otherwise healthy. Even if they look fine, an odor in the ears signals a problem and means it's time to call the vet.

A dog's ears should be cleaned regularly; once a week is suggested, and you can do this along with your regular brushing. Using a cotton ball or pad, and never probing into the ear canal, wipe the ear gently. You can use an ear-cleansing liquid or powder available from your vet or pet-supply store, or some owners prefer to use home-made solutions with ingredients like one-part white vinegar and one-part hydrogen peroxide. Ask your vet about home remedies before you attempt to concoct something on your own!

Keep your dog's ears free of excess hair by plucking it as needed. If done gently, this will be painless for the dog. Look for wax, brown droppings (a sign of ear mites), redness or any other abnormalities. At the first sign of a problem, contact your vet so that he can prescribe an appropriate medication.

EXERCISE

We all know the importance of exercise for humans, so it should come as no surprise that it is essential for our canine friends as

---

SCOOTING HIS BOTTOM

Here's a doggy problem that many owners tend to neglect. If your dog is scooting his rear end around the carpet, he probably is experiencing anal-sac impaction or blockage. The anal sacs are the two grape-sized glands on either side of the dog's vent. The dog cannot empty these glands, which become filled with a foul-smelling material. The dog may attempt to lick the area to relieve the pressure. He may also rub his anus on your walls, furniture or floors.

Don't neglect your dog's rear end during grooming sessions. By squeezing both sides of the anus with a soft cloth, you can express some of the material in the sacs. If the material is pasty and thick, you likely will need the assistance of a veterinarian. Vets know how to express the glands and can show you how to do it correctly without hurting the dog or spraying yourself with poop.

---

well. Now, regardless of your own level of fitness, get ready to assume the role of personal trainer for your dog. It's not as hard as it sounds, and it will have health benefits for you, too.

Just as with anything you do with your dog, you must set a routine for his exercise. It's the same as your going on a run each morning before work or never missing the 7 p.m. aerobics class. If you plan it and get into the habit of actually doing it, it will become just another part of your day. Think of it as making daily exercise appointments with your dog, and stick to your schedule.

As a rule, dogs in normal health should have at least a half-hour of activity each day. Dogs with health or orthopedic problems may have specific limitations and their exercise plans are best devised with the help of a vet. For healthy dogs, there are many ways to fit 30 minutes of activity into your day. Depending on your schedule, you may plan a 15-minute walk or activity session in the morning or again in the evening, or do it all at once in a half-hour session each day. Walking is the most popular way to exercise a dog (it's good for you, too!); other suggestions include retrieving games, jogging and Frisbee® or other active games with his toys. If you have a safe body of water nearby and a dog that likes to swim, swimming is an excellent form of exercise for dogs, putting no stress on his frame.

On that note, some precautions should be taken with a puppy's exercise. During his first year, when he is growing and developing, he should not be subject to stressful activity that stresses his body. Short walks at a comfortable pace and play sessions in the yard are good for a growing pup, and his exercise can be increased as he grows up.

For overweight dogs, dietary changes and activity will help the goal of weight loss (Sound familiar?). While they should of course be encouraged to be active, remember not to overdo it, as the excess weight is already putting strain on his vital organs and bones. As for active and working dogs, some of them never seem to tire! They will enjoy time spent with their owners doing things together.

Regardless of your dog's condition and activity level, exercise offers benefits to all dogs and owners. Consider the fact that dogs who are kept active are more stimulated both physically and mentally, meaning that they are less apt to become bored and lapse into destructive behavior. Also consider the benefits of one-on-one time with your dog every day, continually strengthening the bond between the two of you. Furthermore, exercising together

PUPPY STEPS

Puppies are brimming with activity and enthusiasm. It seems as if they can play all day and night without tiring, but don't overdo your puppy's exercise regimen. Easy does it for the puppy's first six to nine months. Keep walks brief and don't let the puppy engage in stressful jumping games. The puppy frame is delicate, and too much exercise during those critical growing months can cause injury to his bone structure, ligaments and musculature. Save his first jog for his first birthday!

will improve health and longevity for both of you. Both of you need exercise, and now you have a workout partner and motivator!

IDENTIFICATION FOR YOUR SCOTTISH TERRIER

You love your dog and want to keep him safe. Of course you take every precaution to prevent his escaping from the yard or becoming lost or stolen. You have a sturdy high fence and you always keep your dog on-lead when out and about in public places. However, if your dog is not properly identified, you are overlooking a major aspect of his safety. We hope to never be in a situation where our dog is missing, but we should practice prevention in the unfortunate case that this happens; identification greatly increases the chances of your dog's being returned to you.

There are several ways to identify your dog. First, the traditional dog tag should be a staple in your dog's wardrobe, attached to his everyday collar. Tags can be made of sturdy plastic and various metals, and should include your contact information so that a person who finds the dog can get in touch with you right away to arrange his return. Many people today enjoy the wide range of decorative tags available, so have fun and create a tag to match your dog's personality. Of course, it is important that the tag stays on the collar, so have a secure "O" ring attachment; you also can explore the type of tag that slides right onto the collar.

In addition to the ID tag, which every dog should wear even if identified by another method, two other forms of identification have become popular: microchipping and tattooing. In microchipping, a tiny scannable chip is painlessly inserted under the dog's skin. The number is registered to you so that, if your lost dog turns up at a clinic or shelter, the chip can be scanned to retrieve your contact information.

The advantage of the microchip is that it is a permanent form of ID, but there are some factors to consider. Several different companies make microchips, and not all are compatible with the others' scanning devices. It's best to find a company with a universal microchip that can be read by scanners made by other companies as well. It won't do any good to have the dog chipped if the information cannot be retrieved. Also, not every humane society, shelter and clinic is equipped with a scanner, although more and more facilities are equipping themselves. In fact, many shelters microchip dogs that they adopt out to new homes.

In the US, there are five or six major microchip manufacturers as well as a few databases. The American Kennel Club's Companion Animal Recovery unit works in conjunction with HomeAgain™ Companion Animal

Retrieval System (Schering-Plough). In the UK, The Kennel Club is affiliated with the National Pet Register, operated by Wood Green Animal Shelters.

Because the microchip is not visible to the eye, the dog must wear a tag that states that he is microchipped so that whoever picks him up will know to have him scanned. He of course also should have a tag with contact information in case his chip cannot be read. Humane societies and veterinary clinics offer this service, which is usually very affordable.

Though less popular than microchipping, tattooing is another permanent method of ID for dogs. Most vets perform this service, and there are also clinics that perform dog tattooing. This is also an affordable procedure and one that will not cause much discomfort for the dog. It is best to put the tattoo in a visible area, such as the ear, to deter theft. It is sad to say that there are cases of dogs' being stolen and sold to research laboratories, but such laboratories will not accept tattooed dogs.

To ensure that the tattoo is effective in aiding your dog's return to you, the tattoo number must be registered with a national organization. This way, when someone finds a tattooed dog, a phone call to the registry will quickly match the dog with his owner.

This Scottish clan appears well cared for and content.

SMILE WHEN YOU ORDER ME AROUND!

While trainers recommend practicing with your dog every day, it's perfectly acceptable to take a "mental health day" off. It's better not to train the dog on days when you're in a sour mood. Your bad attitude or lack of interest will be sensed by your dog, and he will respond accordingly. Studies show that dogs are well tuned in to their humans' emotions. Be conscious of how you use your voice when talking to your dog. Raising your voice or shouting will only erode your dog's trust in you as his trainer and master.

BASIC TRAINING PRINCIPLES: PUPPY VS. ADULT

There's a big difference between training an adult dog and training a young puppy. With a young puppy, everything is new! At eight to ten weeks of age, he will be experiencing many new things, and he has nothing to which to compare these experiences. Up to this point, he has been with his dam and littermates, not one-on-one with people except in his interactions with his breeder and visitors to the litter.

When you first bring the puppy home, he is eager to please you. This means that he accepts doing things your way! During the next couple of months, he will absorb the basis of everything he needs to know for the rest of his life. This early age is even referred to as the "sponge" stage. After that, for the next 18 months, it's up to you to reinforce good manners by building on the foundation that you've established. Once your puppy is reliable in basic commands and behavior, and has reached the appropriate age, you may gradually introduce him to some of the interesting sports, games

WHO'S TRAINING WHOM?

Dog training is a black-and-white exercise. The correct response to a command must be absolute, and the trainer must insist on completely accurate responses from the dog. A trainer cannot command his dog to sit and settle for the dog's melting into the down position. Often owners are so pleased that their dogs "did something" in response to a command that they just shrug and say, "OK, down" even though they wanted the dog to sit. You want your dog to respond to the command without hesitation: he must respond at that moment and correctly every time.

and activities available to pet owners and their dogs.

Raising your puppy is a family affair. Each member of the family must know what rules to set forth for the puppy and how to use the same one-word commands to mean exactly the same thing every time. Even if yours is a large family, one person will soon be considered by the pup to be the leader, the Alpha person in his pack, the "boss" who must be obeyed. Often that highly regarded person turns out to be the one who feeds the puppy. Food ranks very high on the puppy's list of important things! That's why your puppy is rewarded with small treats along with verbal praise when he

responds to you correctly. As the puppy learns to do what you want him to do, the food rewards are gradually eliminated and only the praise remains. If you keep up with the food treats, you could have two problems on your hands—an obese dog and a beggar.

Training begins the minute your puppy steps through the doorway of your home, so don't make the mistake of putting the puppy on the floor and telling him by your actions, "Go for it! Run wild!" Even if this is your first puppy, you must act like you know what you're doing: be the boss. An uncertain pup may be terrified to move, while a bold one will be ready to take you at your word and start plotting to destroy the house! Before you collected your puppy, you decided where his own special place would be, and that's where to put him when you first arrive home. Give him a house tour after he has investi-gated his area and had a nap and a bathroom "pit stop."

It's worth mentioning here that if you've adopted an adult dog that is completely trained to your liking, lucky you! You're off the hook! However, if that dog spent his life up to this point in a kennel, or even in a good home but without any real training, be prepared to tackle the job ahead. A dog three years of age or older with no previous training cannot

be blamed for not knowing what he was never taught. While the dog is trying to understand and learn your rules, at the same time he has to unlearn many of his previously self-taught habits and general view of the world.

Working with a professional trainer will speed up your progress with an adopted adult dog. You'll need patience, too. Some new rules may be close to impossible for the dog to accept. After all, he's been successful so far by doing everything his way! (Patience again.) He may agree with your instruction for a few days and then slip back into his old ways, so you must be just as consistent and understanding in your teaching as you would be with a puppy. (More patience needed yet again!) Your dog has to learn to pay attention to your voice, your family, the daily routine, new smells, new sounds and, in some cases, even a new climate.

One of the most important things to find out about a newly adopted adult dog is his reaction to children (yours and others), strangers and your friends, and how he acts upon meeting other dogs. If he was not socialized with dogs as a puppy, this could be a major problem. This does not mean that he's a "bad" dog, a vicious dog or an aggressive dog; rather, it means that he has no idea how to read another dog's body language. There's no way for him to tell if the other dog is a friend or foe. Survival instinct takes over, telling him to attack first and ask questions later. This definitely calls for professional help and, even then, may not be a behavior that can be corrected 100% reliably (or even at all). If you have a puppy, this is why it is so very important to introduce your young puppy properly to other puppies and "dog-friendly" adult dogs.

HOUSE-TRAINING

Dogs are tactile-oriented when it comes to house-training. In other words, they respond to the surface on which they are given approval to eliminate. The choice is yours (the dog's version is in parentheses): The lawn (including the neighbors' lawns)? A bare patch of earth under a tree (where people like to sit and relax in the summertime)? Concrete steps or patio (all sidewalks, garage and basement floors)? The curbside (watch out for cars)? A small area of crushed stone in a corner of the yard (mine!)? The latter is the best choice if you can manage it because it will remain strictly for the dog's use and is easy to keep clean.

You can start out with paper-training indoors and switch over to an outdoor surface as the puppy matures and gains control over his need to eliminate. For the

POTTY COMMAND
Most dogs love to please their masters and there are no bounds to what dogs will do to make their owners happy. The potty command is a good example of this theory. If toileting on command makes the master happy, then more power to him. Puppies will obligingly piddle if it really makes their keepers smile. Some owners can be creative about which word they will use to command their dogs to relieve themselves. Some popular choices are "Potty," "Tinkle," "Piddle," "Let's go," "Hurry up" and "Toilet." Give the command every time your puppy goes into position and the puppy will begin to associate his business with the command.

nay-sayers, don't worry—this won't mean that the dog will soil on every piece of newspaper lying around the house. You are training him to go outside, remember? Starting out by paper-training often is the only choice for a city dog.

WHEN YOUR PUPPY'S "GOT TO GO"
Your puppy's need to relieve himself is seemingly non-stop, but signs of improvement will be seen each week. From 8 to 10 weeks old, the puppy will have to be taken outside every time he wakes up, about 10-15 minutes after every meal and after every period of play—all day long, from first thing in the morning until his bedtime! That's a total of ten or

Reinforce training commands at mealtimes. Command your Scottie to sit-stay before you give him his bowl.

DAILY SCHEDULE
How many relief trips does your puppy need per day? A puppy up to the age of 14 weeks will need to go outside about 8 to 12 times per day! You will have to take the pup out any time he starts sniffing around the floor or turning in small circles, as well as after naps, meals, games and lessons or whenever he's released from his crate. Once the puppy is 14 to 22 weeks of age, he will only require 6 to 8 relief trips. At the ages of 22 to 32 weeks, the puppy will require about 5 to 7 trips. Adult dogs typically require 4 relief trips per day, in the morning, afternoon, evening and late at night.

more trips per day to teach the puppy where it's okay to relieve himself. With that schedule in mind, you can see that house-training a young puppy is not a part-time job. It requires someone to be home all day.

If that seems overwhelming or impossible, do a little planning. For example, plan to pick up your puppy at the start of a vacation period. If you can't get home in the middle of the day, plan to hire a dog-sitter or ask a neighbor to come over to take the pup outside, feed him his lunch and then take him out again about ten or so minutes after he's eaten. Also make arrangements with that or another person to be your "emergency" contact if you have to stay late on the job. Remind yourself—repeatedly—that this hectic schedule improves as the puppy gets older.

HOME WITHIN A HOME

Your puppy needs to be confined to one secure, puppy-proof area when no one is able to watch his every move. Generally, the kitchen is the place of choice because the floor is washable. Likewise, it's a busy family area that will accustom the pup to a variety of noises, everything from pots and pans to the telephone, blender and dishwasher. He will also be enchanted by the smell of your cooking (and will never be critical when you burn something). An exercise pen (also called an "ex-pen," a puppy version of a playpen) within the room of choice is an excellent means of confinement for a young pup. He can see out and has a certain amount of space in which to run about, but he is safe from dangerous things like electrical cords, heating units, trash baskets or open kitchen-supply cabinets. Place the pen where the puppy will not get a blast of heat or air conditioning.

In the pen, you can put a few toys, his bed (which can be his crate if the dimensions of pen and crate are compatible) and a few layers of newspaper in one small corner, just in case. A water bowl can be hung at a convenient

BOOT CAMP
Even if one member of the family assumes the role of "drill sergeant," every member of the family has to know what's involved in the dog's education. Success depends on consistency and knowing what words to use, how to use them, how to say them and, most important to the dog, how to praise. The dog will be happy to respond to all members of the family, but don't make the little guy think he's in boot camp!

height on the side of the ex-pen so it won't become a splashing pool for an innovative puppy. His food dish can go on the floor, next to the water bowl.

Crates are something that pet owners are at last getting used to for their dogs. Wild or domestic canines have always preferred to sleep in den-like safe spots, and that is exactly what the crate

Site your Scottie's crate in a central location in your home; a kitchen or sitting room is ideal.

provides. How often have you seen adult dogs that choose to sleep under a table or chair even though they have full run of the house? It's the den connection.

The crate can be solid (fiberglass) with ventilation on the upper sides and a wire-grate door that locks securely, or it can be of open wire construction with a solid floor. Your puppy will go along with whichever one you prefer. The open wire crate, however, should be covered at night to give the snug feeling of a den. A blanket or towel over the top will be fine.

The crate should be big enough for the adult dog to stand up and turn around in, even though he may spend much of his time curled up in the back part of it. There are movable barriers that fit inside dog crates to provide the right amount of space for small puppies that grow into large dogs.

Never afford a young puppy too much space, thinking that you're being kind and generous. He'll just sleep at one end of the crate and soil in the other end! While you should purchase only one crate, one that will accommodate your pup when grown, you will need to make use of the partitions so that the pup has a comfortable area without enough extra space to use as a toilet. A dog does not like to soil where he sleeps, so you are teaching him to "hold it" until it's time for a trip outside. You may want an extra crate to keep in the car for safe traveling.

In your "happy" voice, use the word "Crate" every time you put the pup in his den. If he's new to a crate, toss in a small biscuit for him to chase the first few times. At night, after he's been outside, he should sleep in his crate. The crate may be kept in his designated area at night or, if you want to be sure to hear those wake-up yips in the morning, put the crate in a corner of your bedroom. However, don't make any response whatsoever to whining or crying. If he's completely ignored, he'll settle down and get to sleep.

Good bedding for a young puppy is an old folded bath towel or an old blanket, something that is easily washable and disposable if necessary ("accidents" will happen!). Never put newspaper in the puppy's crate. Those old ideas

CANINE DEVELOPMENT SCHEDULE

It is important to understand how and at what age a puppy develops into adulthood. If you are a puppy owner, consult the following Canine Development Schedule to determine the stage of development your puppy is currently experiencing. This knowledge will help you as you work with the puppy in the weeks and months ahead.

PERIOD	AGE	CHARACTERISTICS
FIRST TO THIRD	BIRTH TO SEVEN WEEKS	Puppy needs food, sleep and warmth and responds to simple and gentle touching. Needs mother for security and disciplining. Needs littermates for learning and interacting with other dogs. Pup learns to function within a pack and learns pack order of dominance. Begin socializing pup with adults and children for short periods. Pup begins to become aware of his environment.
FOURTH	EIGHT TO TWELVE WEEKS	Brain is fully developed. Pup needs socializing with outside world. Remove from mother and littermates. Needs to change from canine pack to human pack. Human dominance necessary. Fear period occurs between 8 and 12 weeks. Avoid fright and pain.
FIFTH	THIRTEEN TO SIXTEEN WEEKS	Training and formal obedience should begin. Less association with other dogs, more with people, places, situations. Period will pass easily if you remember this is pup's change-to-adolescence time. Be firm and fair. Flight instinct prominent. Permissiveness and over-disciplining can do permanent damage. Praise for good behavior.
JUVENILE	FOUR TO EIGHT MONTHS	Another fear period about 7 to 8 months of age. It passes quickly, but be cautious of fright and pain. Sexual maturity reached. Dominant traits established. Dog should understand sit, down, come and stay by now.

NOTE: THESE ARE APPROXIMATE TIME FRAMES. ALLOW FOR INDIVIDUAL DIFFERENCES IN PUPPIES.

CREATURES OF HABIT

Canine behaviorists and trainers aptly describe dogs as "creatures of habit," meaning that dogs respond to structure in their daily lives and welcome a routine. Do not interpret this to mean that dogs enjoy endless repetition in their training sessions. Dogs get bored just as humans do. Keep training sessions interesting and exciting. Vary the commands and the locations in which you practice. Give short breaks for play in between lessons. A bored student will never be the best performer in the class.

of adding a clock to replace his mother's heartbeat, or a hot-water bottle to replace her warmth, are just that—old ideas. The clock could drive the puppy nuts, and the hot-water bottle could end up as a very soggy waterbed! An extremely good breeder would have introduced your puppy to the crate by letting two pups sleep together for a couple of nights, followed by several nights alone. How thankful you will be if you found that breeder!

Safe toys in the pup's crate or area will keep him occupied, but monitor their condition closely. Discard any toys that show signs of being chewed to bits. Squeaky parts, bits of stuffing or plastic or any other small pieces can cause intestinal blockage or possibly choking if swallowed.

PROGRESSING WITH POTTY-TRAINING

After you've taken your puppy out and he has relieved himself in the area you've selected, he can have some free time with the family as long as there is someone responsible for watching him. That doesn't mean just someone in the same room who is watching TV or busy on the computer, but one person who is doing nothing other than keeping an eye on the pup, playing with him on the floor and helping him understand his position in the pack.

This first taste of freedom will let you begin to set the house rules. If you don't want the dog on the furniture, now is the time to prevent his first attempts to jump up onto the couch. The word to use in this case is "Off," not "Down." "Down" is the word you will use to teach the down position, which is something entirely different.

Most corrections at this stage come in the form of simply distracting the puppy. Instead of telling him "No" for "Don't chew the carpet," distract the chomping puppy with a toy and he'll forget about the carpet.

As you are playing with the pup, do not forget to watch him closely and pay attention to his body language. Whenever you see him begin to circle or sniff, take the puppy outside to relieve himself. If you are paper-training,

EXTRA! EXTRA!

The headlines read: "Puppy Piddles Here!" Breeders commonly use newspapers to line their whelping pens, thus puppies learn to associate newspapers with relieving themselves. Do not use newspapers to line your pup's crate, as this will signal to your puppy that it is OK to urinate in his crate. If you choose to paper-train your puppy, you will layer newspapers on a section of the floor near the door he uses to go outside. You should encourage the puppy to use the papers to relieve himself, and bring him there whenever you see him getting ready to go. Little by little, you will reduce the size of the newspaper-covered area so that the puppy will learn to relieve himself "on the other side of the door."

new clean papers, as the scent will attract him to that spot when it's time to go again. That scent attraction is why it's so important to clean up any messes made in the house with a product specially made to eliminate the odor of dog urine and droppings. Regular household cleansers won't do the trick. Pet shops sell the best pet deodorizers. Invest in the largest container you can find.

Scent attraction eventually will lead your pup to his chosen spot outdoors, too; this is the basis of outdoor training. When you take your puppy outside to relieve himself, use a one-word command such as "Outside" or "Go-potty" (that's one word to the

Off-lead heel practice should only be attempted once your dog has mastered his on-lead work.

put him back in his confined area on the newspapers. In either case, praise him as he eliminates, while he actually is in the act of relieving himself. Three seconds after he has finished is too late! You'll be praising him for running toward you, or picking up a toy or whatever he may be doing at that moment, and that's not what you want to be praising him for. Timing is a vital tool in all dog training. Use it!

Remove soiled newspapers immediately and replace them with clean ones. You may want to take a small piece of soiled paper and place it in the middle of the

puppy!) as you pick him up and attach his leash. Then put him down in his area. If for any reason you can't carry him, snap the leash on quickly and lead him to his spot. Now comes the hard part—hard for you, that is. Just stand there until he urinates and defecates. Move him a few feet in one direction or another if he's just sitting there looking at you, but remember that this is neither playtime nor time for a walk. This is strictly a business trip! Then, as he circles and squats (remember your timing!), give him a quiet "Good dog" as praise. If you start to jump for joy, ecstatic over his performance, he'll do one of two things: either he will stop mid-stream, as it were, or he'll do it again for you—in the house—and expect you to be just as delighted!

Give him five minutes or so

> ### TIDY BOY
> Clean by nature, dogs do not like to soil their dens, which in effect are their crates or sleeping quarters. Unless not feeling well, dogs will not defecate or urinate in their crates. Crate training capitalizes on the dog's natural desire to keep his den clean. Be conscientious about giving the puppy as many opportunities to relieve himself outdoors as possible. Reward the puppy for correct behavior. Praise him and pat his head whenever he "goes" in the correct location. Even the tidiest of puppies can have potty accidents, so be patient and dedicate more energy to helping your puppy achieve a clean lifestyle.

and, if he doesn't go in that time, take him back indoors to his confined area and try again in

When housebreaking your Scottie, lead him to the same spot every time he requires relief.

another ten minutes, or immediately if you see him sniffing and circling. By careful observation, you'll soon work out a successful schedule.

Accidents, by the way, are just that—accidents. Clean them up quickly and thoroughly, without comment, after the puppy has been taken outside to finish his business and then put back in his area or crate. If you witness an accident in progress, say "No!" in a stern voice and get the pup outdoors immediately. No punishment is needed. You and your puppy are just learning each other's language and sometimes it's easy to miss a puppy's message. Chalk it up to experience and watch more closely from now on.

KEEPING THE PACK ORDERLY

Discipline is a form of training that brings order to life. For example, military discipline is what allows the soldiers in an army to work as one. Discipline is a form of teaching and, in dogs, is the basis of how the successful pack operates. Each member knows his place in the pack and all respect the leader, or Alpha dog. It is essential for your puppy that you establish this type of relationship, with you as the Alpha, or leader. It is a form of social coexistence that all canines recognize and accept. Discipline, therefore, is never to be confused

LEASH TRAINING

House-training and leash training go hand in hand, literally. When taking your puppy outside to do his business, lead him there on his leash. Unless an emergency potty run is called for, do not whisk the puppy in your arms and take him outside. If you have a fenced yard, you have the advantage of letting the puppy loose to go out, but it's better to put the dog on the leash and take him to his designated place in the yard until he is reliably house-trained. Taking the puppy for a walk is the best way to house-train a dog. The dog will associate the walk with his time to relieve himself and the exercise of walking stimulates the dog's bowels and bladder. Dogs that are not trained to relieve themselves on a walk may hold it until they get back home, which of course defeats half the purpose of the walk.

with punishment. When you teach your puppy how you want him to behave, and he behaves properly and you praise him for it, you are disciplining him with a form of positive reinforcement.

For a dog, rewards come in the form of praise, a smile, a cheerful tone of voice, a few friendly pats or a rub of the ears. Rewards are also small food treats. Obviously, that does not mean bits of regular dog food. Rather, treats are very small bits of special things like cheese or pieces of soft dog treats. The idea is to reward the dog with something very small that he can taste and swallow, providing instant positive reinforcement. If he has to take time to chew the treat, by the time he is finished, he will have forgotten what he did to earn it!

Your puppy should never be physically punished. The displeasure shown on your face and in your voice is sufficient to signal to the pup that he has done something wrong. He wants to please everyone higher up on the social ladder, especially his leader, so a scowl and harsh voice will take care of the error. Growling out the word "Shame!" when the pup is caught in the act of doing something wrong is better than the repetitive "No." Some dogs hear "No" so often that they begin to think it's their name! By the way, do not use the dog's name when you're correcting him. His name is reserved to get his attention for something pleasant about to take place.

There are punishments that have nothing to do with you. For

SHOULD WE ENROLL?
If you have the means and the time, you should definitely take your dog to obedience classes. Begin with Kindergarten Puppy Classes in which puppies of all sizes learn basic lessons while getting the opportunity to meet and greet each other; it's as much about socialization as it is about good manners. What you learn in class, you can practice at home. And if you goof up in practice, you'll get help in the next session.

example, your dog may think that chasing cats is one reason for his existence. You can try to stop it as much as you like without success because it's such fun for the dog. But one good hissing, spitting, swipe of a cat's claws across the dog's nose will put an end to the game forever. Only intervene when you're dog's eyeball is seriously at risk. Cat scratches can cause permanent damage to an innocent but annoying puppy.

PUPPY KINDERGARTEN

COLLAR AND LEASH
Before you begin your puppy's education, he must be used to his collar and leash. Choose a collar for your puppy that is secure, but not heavy or bulky. He won't enjoy training if he's uncomfortable. A flat buckle collar is fine for everyday wear and for initial

puppy training. For older dogs, there are several types of training collars such as the martingale, which is a double loop that tightens slightly around the neck, or the head collar, which is similar to a horse's halter. Do not use a chain choke collar unless you have been specifically shown how to put it on and how to use it. Small breeds and coated breeds are not suitable for chain chokes.

A lightweight 6-foot woven cotton or nylon training leash is preferred by most trainers because it is easy to fold up in your hand and comfortable to hold because there is a certain amount of give to it. There are lessons where the dog will start off six feet away from you at the end of the leash. The leash used to take the puppy outside to relieve himself is shorter because you don't want him to roam away from his area. The shorter leash will also be the one to use when you walk the puppy for the same reason.

If you've been fortunate enough to enroll in a Kindergarten Puppy Training class, suggestions will be made as to the best collar and leash for your young puppy. We say "fortunate" because your puppy will be in a class with puppies in his age range (up to five months old) of all breeds and sizes. It's the perfect way for him to learn the right way (and the wrong way) to interact with other dogs as well as their people. You

NO MORE TREATS!
When your dog is responding promptly and correctly to commands, it's time to eliminate treats. Begin by alternating a treat reward with a verbal-praise-only reward. Gradually eliminate all treats while increasing the frequency of praise. Overlook pleading eyes and expectant expressions, but if he's still watching your treat hand, you're on your way to using hand signals.

Once your Scottie has mastered the basic sit exercise, you can practice the command from greater distances and off-lead.

cannot teach your puppy how to interpret another dog's sign language. For a first-time puppy owner, these socialization classes are invaluable. For experienced dog owners, they are a real boon to further training.

ATTENTION

You've been using the dog's name since the minute you collected him from the breeder, so you should be able to get his attention by saying his name—with a big smile and in an excited tone of voice. His response will be the puppy equivalent of "Here I am! What are we going to do?" Your immediate response (if you haven't guessed by now) is "Good dog." Rewarding him at the moment he pays attention to you teaches him the proper way to respond when he hears his name.

EXERCISES FOR A BASIC CANINE EDUCATION

THE SIT EXERCISE

There are several ways to teach the puppy to sit. The first one is

to catch him whenever he is about to sit and, as his backside nears the floor, say "Sit, good dog!" That's positive reinforcement and, if your timing is sharp, he will learn that what he's doing at that second is connected to your saying "Sit" and that you think he's clever for doing it!

Another method is to start with the puppy on his leash in front of you. Show him a treat in the palm of your right hand. Bring your hand up under his nose and, almost in slow motion, move your hand up and back so his nose goes up in the air and his head tilts back as he follows the treat in your hand. At that point, he will have to either sit or fall over, so as

HOW DO YOU GET TO CARNEGIE HALL?

Or the National Obedience Championships? The same way you get your dog to do anything – practice, practice, practice. It's how you practice that counts. Keep sessions short, varied, interesting and interspersed with active fun. A bored dog isn't learning. If you're feeling out of sorts yourself, quit for the day. Set yourself a reasonable schedule for several brief practice sessions every day and stick to it. Practice randomly throughout the day as you're doing different things around the house. Lots of praise for that good "Sit" in front of the TV or while waiting for his dinner!

his back legs buckle under, say "Sit, good dog," and then give him the treat and lots of praise. You may have to begin with your hand lightly running up his chest, actually lifting his chin up until he sits. Some large (and usually older) dogs require gentle pressure on their hindquarters with the left

RIGHT CLICK ON YOUR DOG

With three clicks, the dolphin jumps through the hoop. Wouldn't it be nice to have a dog who could obey wordless commands that easily? Clicker training actually was developed by dolphin trainers and today is used on dogs with great success. You can buy a clicker at a pet shop or pet-supply outlet, and then you'll be off and clicking.

You can click your dog into learning new commands, shaping or conditioning his behavior and solving bad habits. The clicker, used in conjunction with a treat, is an extension of positive reinforcement. The dog begins to recognize your happy clicking and you will never have to use physical force again. The dog is conditioned to follow your hand with the clicker, just as he would follow your hand with a treat. To discourage the dog from inappropriate behavior (like jumping up or barking), you can use the clicker to set a timeframe and then click and reward the dog once he's waited the allotted time without jumping up or barking.

hand, in which case the dog should be on your left side. Puppies generally do not appreciate this physical dominance.

After a few times, you should be able to show the dog a treat in the open palm of your hand, raise your hand waist-high as you say "Sit" and have him sit. Once again, you have taught him two things at the same time. The verbal command and the motion of the hand are both signals for the sit. Your puppy is watching you almost more than he is listening to you, so what you do is just as important as what you say.

Don't save any of these drills only for training sessions. Use them as much as possible at odd

No matter how well trained your Scottie is, a tasty treat still retains its magical power.

times during a normal day. The dog should always sit before being given his food dish. He should sit to let you go through a doorway first, when the doorbell rings or when you stop to speak to someone on the street.

THE DOWN EXERCISE

Before beginning to teach the down command, you must consider how the dog feels about this exercise. To him, "down" is a submissive position. Being flat on the floor with you standing over him is not his idea of fun. It's up to you to let him know that, while it may not be fun, the reward of your approval is worth his effort.

Start with the puppy on your left side in a sit position. Hold the leash right above his collar in your left hand. Have an extra-special treat, such as a small piece of cooked chicken or hot dog, in your right hand. Place it at the end of the pup's nose and steadily move your hand down and forward along the ground. Hold the leash to prevent a sudden lunge for the food. As the puppy goes into the down position, say "Down" very gently.

The difficulty with this exercise is twofold: it's both the submissive aspect and the fact that most people say the word "Down" as if they were a drill sergeant in charge of recruits! So issue the command sweetly, give him the treat and have the pup

DOWN

"Down" is a harsh-sounding word and a submissive posture in dog body language, thus presenting two obstacles in teaching the down command. When the dog is about to flop down on his own, tell him "Good down." Pups that are not good about being handled learn better by lowering food in front of them. A dog that has your trust can be gently guided into position. When you give the command "Down," be sure to say it sweetly!

maintain the down position for several seconds. If he tries to get up immediately, place your hands on his shoulders and press down gently, giving him a very quiet "Good dog." As you progress with this lesson, increase the "down time" until he will hold it until you say "Okay" (his cue for release). Practice this one in the house at various times throughout the day.

By increasing the length of time during which the dog must maintain the down position, you'll find many uses for it. For example, he can lie at your feet in the vet's office or anywhere that both of you have to wait, when you are on the phone, while the family is eating and so forth. If you progress to training for competitive obedience, he'll already be all set for the exercise called the "long down."

Stay is an important exercise and can readily be taught if you have patience and persistence.

THE STAY EXERCISES

To teach the sit/stay, have the dog sit on your left side. Hold the leash at waist level in your left hand and let the dog know that you have a treat in your closed right hand. Step forward on your right foot as you say "Stay." Immediately turn and stand directly in front of the dog, keeping your right hand up high so he'll keep his eye on the treat hand and maintain the sit position for a count of five. Return to your original position and offer the reward.

Increase the length of the sit/stay each time until the dog can hold it for at least 30 seconds without moving. After about a week of success, move out on your right foot and take two steps

---

OKAY!

This is the signal that tells your dog that he can quit whatever he was doing. Use "Okay" to end a session on a correct response to a command. (Never end on an incorrect response.) Lots of praise follows. People use "Okay" a lot and it has other uses for dogs, too. Your dog is barking. You say, "Okay! Come!" "Okay" signals him to stop the barking activity and "Come" allows him to come to you for a "Good dog."

before turning to face the dog. Give the "Stay" hand signal (left palm back toward the dog's head) as you leave. He gets the treat when you return and he holds the sit/stay. Increase the distance that you walk away from him before turning until you reach the length of your training leash. But don't rush it! Go back to the beginning if he moves before he should. No matter what the lesson, never be upset by having to back up for a few days. The repetition and practice are what will make your dog reliable in these commands. It won't do any good to move on to something more difficult if the command is not mastered at the easier levels. Above all, even if you do get frustrated, never let your puppy know! Always keep a positive, upbeat attitude during training, which will transmit to

COME AND GET IT!

The come command is your dog's safety signal. Until he is 99% perfect in responding, don't use the come command if you cannot enforce it. Practice on leash with treats or squeakers, or whenever the dog is running to you. Never call him to come to you if he is to be corrected for a misdemeanor. Reward the dog with a treat and happy praise whenever he comes to you.

your dog for positive results!

The down/stay is taught in the same way once the dog is completely reliable and steady with the down command. Again, don't rush it. With the dog in the down position on your left side, step out on your right foot as you say "Stay." Return by walking around in back of the dog and into your original position. While you are training, it's okay to murmur something like "Hold on" to encourage him to stay put. When the dog will stay without moving when you are at a distance of 3 or 4 feet, begin to increase the length of time before you return. Be sure he holds the down on your return until you say "Okay." At that point, he gets his treat–just so he'll remember for next time that it's not over until it's over.

THE COME EXERCISE

No command is more important to the safety of your dog than "come." It is what you should say every single time you see the puppy running toward you: "Binky, come! Good dog." During playtime, run a few feet away from the puppy, turn and tell him to "come" as he is already running to you. You can go so far as to teach your puppy two things at once if you squat down and hold out your arms. As the pup gets close to you and you're saying "Good dog," bring your

> **DON'T STRESS ME OUT**
> Your dog doesn't have to deal with paying the bills, the daily commute, PTA meetings and the like, but, believe it or not, there's lots of stress in a dog's world. Stress can be caused by the owner's impatient demeanor and his angry or harsh corrections. If your dog cringes when you reach for his training collar, he's stressed. An older dog is sometimes stressed out when he goes to a new home. No matter what the cause, put off all training until he's over it. If he's going through a fear period— shying away from people, trembling when spoken to, avoiding eye contact or hiding under furniture —wait to resume training. Naturally you'd also postpone your lessons if the dog were sick, and the same goes for you. Be compassionate.

right arm in about waist-high. Now he's also learning the hand signal, an excellent device should you be on the phone when you need to get him to come to you! You'll also both be one step ahead when you enter obedience classes.

Puppies, like children, have notoriously short attention spans, so don't overdo it with any of the training. Keep each lesson short. Break it up with a quick run around the yard or a ball toss, repeat the lesson and quit as soon as the pup gets it right. That way, you will always end with a "Good dog."

When the puppy responds to your well-timed "Come," try it with the puppy on the training leash. This time, catch him off-guard, while he's sniffing a leaf or watching a bird: "Binky, come!" You may have to pause for a split second after his name to be sure you have his attention. If the puppy shows any sign of confusion, give the leash a mild jerk and take a couple of steps backward. Do not repeat the command. In this case, as he reaches you, you should say "Good come!"

That's the number-one rule of training. Each command word is given just once. Anything more is nagging. You'll also notice that all commands are one word only. Even when they are actually two words, you say them as one.

Never call the dog to come to you—with or without his name—

if you are angry or intend to correct him for some misbehavior. When correcting the pup, you go to him. Your dog must always connect "come" with something pleasant and with your approval; then you can rely on his response. Life isn't perfect and neither are puppies. A time will come, often around 10 months of age, when he'll become "selectively deaf" or choose to "forget" his name. He may respond by wagging his tail (and even seeming to smile at you) with a look that says "Make me!" Laugh, throw his favorite toy and skip the lesson you had planned. Pups will be pups!

The Heel Exercise

The second most important command to teach, after the come, is the heel. When you are walking your growing puppy, you need to be in control. Besides, it looks terrible to be pulled and yanked down the street, and it's not much fun either! Your eight-to ten-week old puppy will probably follow you everywhere, but that's his natural instinct, not your control over the situation. However, any time he does follow you, you can say "Heel" and be ahead of the game, as he will learn to associate this command with the action of following you before you even begin teaching him to heel.

There is a very precise, almost military, procedure for teaching your dog to heel. As with all

Still chewing on his leash, this Scottie puppy has a long way to go!

FROM HEEL TO ETERNITY

To begin, step away from the dog, who is in the sit position, on your right foot. That tells the dog you aren't going anywhere. Turn and stand directly in front of him so he won't be tempted to follow. Two seconds is a long, long time to your dog, so only increase the time for which he's expected to stay in short increments. Don't force it. When practicing the heel exercise, your dog will sit at your side whenever you stop. Don't stop for more than three seconds, as your enthusiastic dog will really feel as if it's an eternity!

obedience training, begin with the dog on your left side. He will be in a very nice sit and you will have the training leash across your chest. Hold the loop and folded leash in your right hand. Pick up the slack leash above the dog in your left hand and hold it loosely at your side. Step out on your left foot as you say "Heel." If the puppy does not move, give a gentle tug or pat your left leg to get him started. If he surges ahead of you, stop and pull him back gently until he is at your side. Tell him to sit and begin again.

Walk a few steps and stop while the puppy is correctly beside you. Tell him to sit and give mild verbal praise. (More enthusiastic praise will encourage him to think the lesson is over.) Repeat the lesson, only increasing the number of steps you take as long as the dog is heeling nicely beside you. When you end the lesson, have him hold the sit, then give him the "Okay" to let him know that this is the end of the lesson. Praise him so that he knows he did a good job.

The cure for excessive pulling (a common problem) is to stop when the dog is no more than 2 or 3 feet ahead of you. Guide him back into position and begin again. With a really determined puller, try switching to a head collar. This will automatically turn the pup's head toward you

"Where are you?" Teaching your Scottie to come is easily accomplished by making the exercise into a rewarding, exciting game for your dog.

Don't forget to allow your Scottie to run off some of his post-lesson stress.

so you can bring him back easily to the heel position. Give quiet, reassuring praise every time the leash goes slack and he's staying with you.

Staying and heeling can take a lot out of a dog, so provide playtime and free-running exercise when the lessons are over to shake off the stress. You don't want him to associate training with all work and no fun.

TAPERING OFF TIDBITS

Your dog has been watching you—and the hand that treats—throughout all of his lessons, and now it's time to break the treat habit. Begin by giving him treats at the end of each lesson only. Then start to give a treat after the end of only some of the lessons. At the end of every lesson, as well as during the lessons, be consistent with the praise. Your pup now doesn't know if he'll get a treat or not, but he should keep

performing well just in case! Finally, you will stop giving treat rewards entirely. Save them for something brand-new that you want to teach him. Keep up the praise and you'll always have a "good dog."

OBEDIENCE CLASSES

The advantages of an obedience class are that your dog will have to learn amid the distractions of other people and dogs and that your mistakes will be quickly corrected by the trainer. Teaching your dog along with a qualified instructor and other handlers

---

TIPS FOR TRAINING AND SAFETY

1. On- or off-leash, practice only in a fenced area.
2. Remove the training collar when the training session is over.
3. Don't try to separate a dog-fight.
4. "Come," "Leave it" and "Wait" are safety commands.
5. The dog belongs in a crate or behind a barrier when riding in the car.
6. Don't ignore the dog's first sign of aggression. Aggression only gets worse, so take it seriously.
7. Keep the faces of children and dogs separated.
8. Pay attention to what the dog is chewing.
9. Keep the vet's number near your phone.
10. "Okay" is a useful release command.

MORE PRAISE, LESS FOOD

As you progress with your puppy's lessons, and the puppy is responding well, gradually begin to withhold the treats by alternating the use of treats with times when you offer only verbal praise or a few pats on the dog's side. (Pats on the head are dominant actions and he won't think they are meant to be praise.) Every lesson should end with the puppy's performing the correct action for that session's command. When he gets it right and you withhold the treat, the praise can be as long and lavish as you like. The commands are one word only, but your verbal praise can use as many words as you want...don't skimp!

who may have more dog experience than you is a further plus of the class environment. The instructor and other handlers can help you to find the most efficient way of teaching your dog a command or exercise. It's often easier to learn from other people's mistakes than your own. You will also learn all of the requirements for competitive obedience trials, in which you can earn titles and go on to advanced jumping and retrieving exercises, which are fun for many dogs. Obedience classes build the foundation needed for many other canine activities (in which we humans are allowed to participate, too!).

TRAINING YOUR SCOTTISH TERRIER FOR OTHER ACTIVITIES

Once your dog has basic obedience under his collar, and is 12 months of age, you can enter the world of agility training. Dogs think agility is pure fun, like being turned loose in an amusement park full of obstacles! In addition to agility, there are hunting activities for sporting dogs, lure-coursing events for sighthounds, go-to-ground events for terriers, racing for the Nordic sled dogs, herding trials for the shepherd breeds and tracking, which is open to all "nosey" dogs (which would include all dogs!). For those who like to volunteer, there is the wonderful feeling of owning a Therapy Dog and visiting hospices, nursing homes and veterans' homes to bring smiles, comfort and companionship to those who live there.

Around the house, your dog can be taught to do some simple chores. You might teach him to carry a basket of household items or to fetch the morning newspaper. The kids can teach the dog all kinds of tricks, from playing hide-and-seek to balancing a biscuit on his nose. A family dog is what rounds out the family. Everything he does beyond sitting in your lap or gazing lovingly at you represents the bonus of owning a dog.

HEALTHCARE OF YOUR

SCOTTISH TERRIER

By Lowell Ackerman DVM, DACVD

HEALTHCARE FOR A LIFETIME

When you own a Scottish Terrier, you become his healthcare advocate over his entire lifespan, as well as being the one to shoulder the financial burden of such care. Accordingly, it is worthwhile to focus on prevention rather than treatment, as you and your pet will both be happier.

Of course, the best place to have begun your program of preventative healthcare is with the initial purchase or adoption of your Scottie. There is no way of guaranteeing that your new furry friend is free of medical problems, but there are some things you can do to improve your odds. You certainly should have done adequate research into your breed of choice and have selected your puppy carefully rather than buying on impulse. Health issues aside, a large number of pet abandonment and relinquishment cases arise from a mismatch between

Take your newly acquired Scottie puppy to the veterinarian immediately. Be sure to get the necessary information about the pup's health history from the breeder, including the initial dates of inoculations and the like.

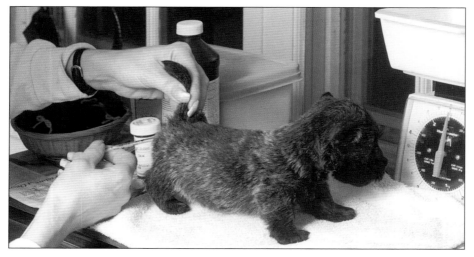

pet needs and owner expectations. This is entirely preventable with appropriate planning and finding a good breeder.

Regarding healthcare issues specifically, it is very difficult to make blanket statements about where to acquire a problem-free pet, but, again, a reputable breeder is your best bet. In an ideal situation, you have the opportunity to see both parents, get references from other owners of the breeder's pups and see genetic-testing documentation for several generations of the litter's ancestors. At the very least, you must thoroughly investigate your breed of interest and the problems inherent in that breed, as well as the genetic testing available to screen for those problems. Genetic testing offers some important benefits, but testing is only available for a few disorders in a relatively small number of breeds and is not available for some of the most common genetic diseases, such as hip dysplasia, cataracts, epilepsy, cardiomyopathy, etc. This area of research is indeed exciting and increasingly important, and advances will continue to be made each year. In fact, recent research has shown that there is an equivalent dog gene for 75% of known human genes, so research done

TAKING YOUR DOG'S TEMPERATURE
It is important to know how to take your dog's temperature at times when you think he may be ill. It's not the most enjoyable task, but can be done without too much difficulty. It's easier with a helper, preferably someone with whom the dog is friendly, so that one of you can hold the dog while the other inserts the thermometer.

Before inserting the thermometer, coat the end with petroleum jelly. Insert the thermometer slowly and gently into the dog's rectum about one inch. Wait for the reading, about two minutes. Be sure to remove the thermometer carefully and clean it thoroughly after each use.

A dog's normal body temperature is between 100.5 and 102.5 degrees F. Immediate veterinary attention is required if the dog's temperature is below 99 or above 104 degrees F.

in either species is likely to benefit the other.

We've also discussed that evaluating your chosen pup's behavioral nature and that of his immediate family members is an important part of the selection process that cannot be underestimated or underemphasized. It is sometimes difficult to evaluate temperament in puppies because certain behavioral tendencies, such as some forms of aggression, may

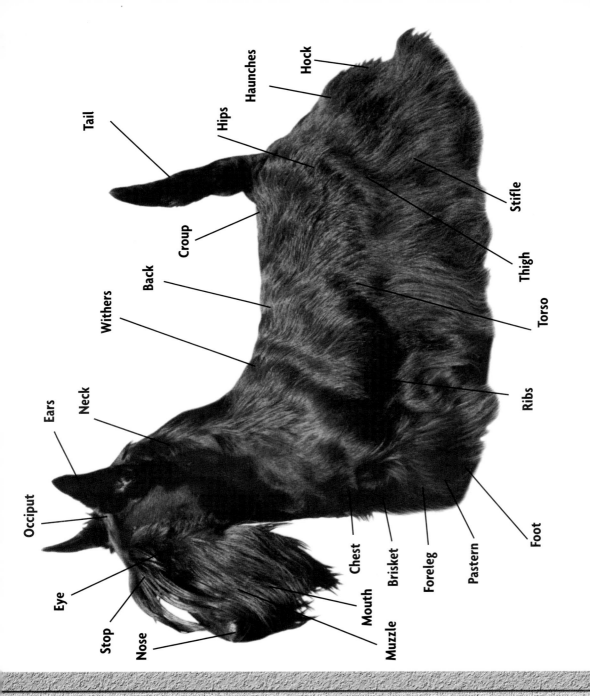

Tail

Haunches

Hock

Hips

Croup

Stifle

Back

Thigh

Withers

Torso

Neck

Ears

Ribs

Occiput

Foot

Eye

Pastern

Stop

Foreleg

Nose

Brisket

Muzzle

Chest

Mouth

PHYSICAL STRUCTURE OF THE SCOTTISH TERRIER

not be immediately evident. More dogs are euthanized each year for behavioral reasons than for all medical conditions combined, so it is critical to take temperament issues seriously. Start with a well-balanced, friendly companion and put the time and effort into proper socialization, and you will both be rewarded with a lifelong valued relationship.

With a pup from healthy, sound stock, you become responsible for helping your veterinarian keep your pet healthy. Some crucial things happen before you even bring your puppy home. Parasite control typically begins at two weeks of age and vaccinations typically begin at six to eight weeks of age. A pre-pubertal evaluation is typically scheduled for about six months

of age. At this time, a dental evaluation is done (since the adult teeth are now in), heartworm prevention is started and neutering or spaying is most commonly done.

It is critical to commence regular dental care at home if you have not already done so. It may not sound so important, but most dogs have active periodontal disease by four years of age if they don't have their teeth cleaned regularly at home, not just at their veteri-nary exams. Dental problems lead to more than just bad "doggie breath": gum disease can have very serious medical consequences. If you start brushing your dog's teeth and using antiseptic rinses from a young age, your dog will be accustomed to it and will not resist. The results will be healthy dentition, which your pet will need to enjoy a long, healthy life.

Most dogs are considered adults at a year of age, although some larger breeds still have some filling out to do up to about two or so years old. Each breed has different healthcare requirements, so work with your veterinarian to determine what will be needed and what your role should be. This doctor-client relationship is important, because as vaccination guidelines change, there may

Before you buy a dog, meet and interview the veterinarians in your area. Take everything into consideration; discuss background, specialties, fees, emergency policies, etc.

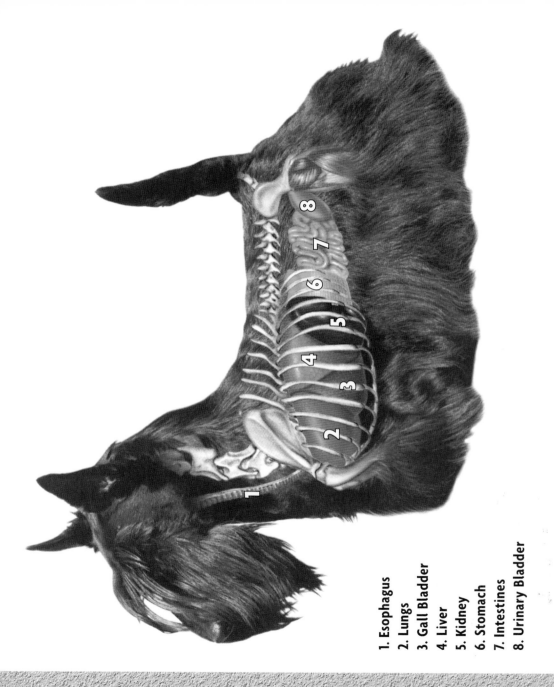

1. Esophagus
2. Lungs
3. Gall Bladder
4. Liver
5. Kidney
6. Stomach
7. Intestines
8. Urinary Bladder

INTERNAL ORGANS OF THE SCOTTISH TERRIER

not be an annual "vaccine visit" scheduled. You must make sure that you see your veterinarian at least annually, even if no vaccines are due, because this is the best opportunity to coordinate healthcare activities and to make sure that no medical issues creep by unaddressed.

When your Scottie reaches three-quarters of his anticipated lifespan, he is considered a "senior" and likely requires some special care. In general, if you've been taking great care of your canine companion throughout his formative and adult years, the transition to senior status should be a smooth one. Age is not a disease, and as

long as everything is functioning as it should, there is no reason why most of late adulthood should not be rewarding for both you and your pet. This is especially true if you have tended to the details, such as regular veterinary visits, proper dental care, excellent nutrition and management of bone and joint issues.

At this stage in your Scottie's life, your veterinarian may want to schedule visits twice yearly, instead of once, to run some laboratory screenings, electrocardiograms and the like, and to change the diet to something more digestible. Catching problems early is the

SAMPLE VACCINATION SCHEDULE

6-8 weeks of age	Parvovirus, Distemper, Adenovirus-2 (Hepatitis)
9-11 weeks of age	Parvovirus, Distemper, Adenovirus-2 (Hepatitis)
12-14 weeks of age	Parvovirus, Distemper, Adenovirus-2 (Hepatitis)
12-16 weeks of age	Rabies
1 year of age	Parvovirus, Distemper, Adenovirus-2 (Hepatitis), Rabies

Revaccination is performed every one to three years, depending on the product, the method of administration and the patient's risk. Initial adult inoculation (for dogs at least 16 weeks of age in which a puppy series was not done or could not be confirmed) is two vaccinations, done three to four weeks apart, with revaccination according to the same criteria mentioned. Other vaccines are given as decided between owner and veterinarian.

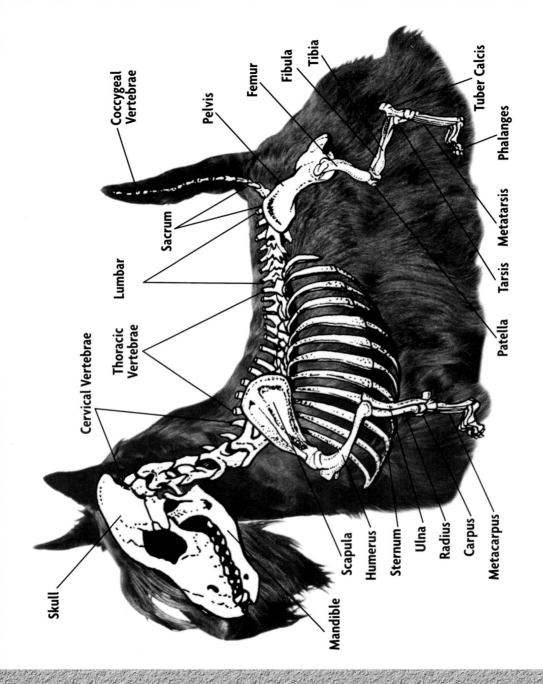

Coccygeal Vertebrae

Pelvis

Femur

Fibula

Tibia

Tuber Calcis

Phalanges

Sacrum

Metatarsis

Lumbar

Tarsis

Thoracic Vertebrae

Patella

Cervical Vertebrae

Scapula

Humerus

Sternum

Ulna

Radius

Carpus

Metacarpus

Skull

Mandible

SKELETAL STRUCTURE OF THE SCOTTISH TERRIER

best way to manage them effectively. Treating the early stages of heart disease is so much easier than trying to intervene when there is more significant damage to the heart muscle. Similarly, managing the beginning of kidney problems is fairly routine if there is no significant kidney damage. Other problems, like cognitive dysfunction (similar to senility and Alzheimer's disease), cancer, diabetes and arthritis, are more common in older dogs, but all can be treated to help the dog live as many happy, comfortable years as possible. Just as in people, medical management is more effective (and less expensive) when you catch things early.

SELECTING A VETERINARIAN

There is probably no more important decision that you will make regarding your pet's healthcare than the selection of his doctor. Your pet's veterinarian will be a pediatrician, family-practice physician and gerontologist, depending on the

DISEASE REFERENCE CHART

	WHAT IS IT?	WHAT CAUSES IT?	SYMPTOMS
Leptospirosis	Severe disease that affects the internal organs; can be spread to people.	A bacterium, which is often carried by rodents, that enters through mucous membranes and spreads quickly throughout the body.	Range from fever, vomiting and loss of appetite in less severe cases to shock, irreversible kidney damage and possibly death in most severe cases.
Rabies	Potentially deadly virus that infects warm-blooded mammals.	Bite from a carrier of the virus, mainly wild animals.	1st stage: dog exhibits change in behavior, fear. 2nd stage: dog's behavior becomes more aggressive. 3rd stage: loss of coordination, trouble with bodily functions.
Parvovirus	Highly contagious virus, potentially deadly.	Ingestion of the virus, which is usually spread through the feces of infected dogs.	Most common: severe diarrhea. Also vomiting, fatigue, lack of appetite.
Canine cough	Contagious respiratory infection.	Combination of types of bacteria and virus. Most common: *Bordetella bronchiseptica* bacteria and parainfluenza virus.	Chronic cough.
Distemper	Disease primarily affecting respiratory and nervous system.	Virus that is related to the human measles virus.	Mild symptoms such as fever, lack of appetite and mucus secretion progress to evidence of brain damage, "hard pad."
Hepatitis	Virus primarily affecting the liver.	Canine adenovirus type I (CAV-1). Enters system when dog breathes in particles.	Lesser symptoms include listlessness, diarrhea, vomiting. More severe symptoms include "blue-eye" (clumps of virus in eye).
Coronavirus	Virus resulting in digestive problems.	Virus is spread through infected dog's feces.	Stomach upset evidenced by lack of appetite, vomiting, diarrhea.

dog's life stage, and will be the individual who makes recommendations regarding issues such as when specialists need to be consulted, when diagnostic testing and/or therapeutic intervention is needed and when you will need to seek outside emergency and critical-care services. Your vet will act as your advocate and liaison throughout these processes.

Everyone has his own idea about what to look for in a vet, an individual who will play a big role in his dog's (and, of course, his own) life for many years to come. For some, it is the compassionate caregiver with whom they hope to develop a professional relationship to span the lifetime of their dogs and even their future pets. For others, they are seeking a clinician with keen diagnostic and therapeutic insight, who can deliver state-of-the-art health care. Still others need a veterinary facility that is open evenings and weekends, or is in close proximity, or provides mobile veterinary services, to accommodate their schedules; these people may not much mind that their dogs might see different veterinarians on each visit. Just as we have different reasons for selecting our own health care professionals (e.g., covered by insurance plan,

expert in field, convenient location, etc.), we should not expect that there is a one-size-fits-all recommendation for

---

YOUR DOG NEEDS TO VISIT THE VET IF:

- He has ingested a toxin such as antifreeze or a toxic plant; in these cases, administer first aid and call the vet right away
- His teeth are discolored, loose or missing or he has sores and/or other signs of infection or abnormality in the mouth
- He has been vomiting, has had diarrhea or has been constipated for over 24 hours, or immediately if you notice blood
- He has refused food for over 24 hours
- His weight, eating habits, water intake and/or toilet habits have noticeably changed; you have noticed weight gain or weight loss
- He shows symptoms of bloat, , which requires immediate attention
- He is salivating excessively
- He has a lump in his throat
- He has a lumps or bumps anywhere on the body
- He is very lethargic
- He appears to be in pain or otherwise has trouble chewing or swallowing
- His skin loses elasticity.

Of course, there will be other instances in which a visit to the vet is necessary; these are just some of the signs that could be indicative of serious problems that need to be caught as early as possible.

PROBLEM: AND THAT STARTS WITH "P"

Urinary tract problems more commonly affect female dogs, especially those who have been spayed. The first sign that a urinary tract problem exists is usually a strong odor from the urine or an unusual color. Blood in the urine, known as hematuria, is another sign of an infection, related to cystitis, a bladder infection, bladder cancer or a blood-clotting disorder. Urinary tract problems can also be signaled by the dog's straining while urinating, experiencing pain during urination and genital discharge as well as excessive water intake and urination.

Excessive drinking, in and of itself, does not indicate a urinary tract problem. A dog who is drinking more than normal may have a kidney or liver problem, a hormonal disorder or diabetes mellitus. Behaviorists report a disorder known as psychogenic polydipsia, which manifests itself in excessive drinking and urination. If you notice your dog drinking much more than normal, take him to the vet.

same, and you will be happiest with one that truly meets your needs.

There is another point to be considered in the selection of veterinary services. Not that long ago, a single veterinarian would attempt to manage all medical and surgical issues as they arose. That was often problematic, because veterinarians are trained in many species and many diseases, and it was just impossible for general veterinary practitioners to be experts in every species, every field and every ailment. However, just as in the human health care fields, specialization has allowed general practitioners to concentrate on primary health care delivery, especially wellness and the prevention of infectious diseases, and to utilize a network of specialists to assist

selecting a veterinarian and veterinary practice. The best advice is to be honest in your assessment of what you expect from a veterinary practice and to conscientiously research the options in your area. You will quickly appreciate that not all veterinary practices are the

Perhaps the best exercise for your Scottie comes from a playmate. This Scottie has an able jogging partner in a black Labrador.

in the management of conditions that require specific expertise and experience. Thus, there are now many types of veterinary specialists, including dermatologists, cardiologists, ophthalmologists, surgeons, internists, oncologists, neurologists, behaviorists, criticalists and others to help primary-care veterinarians deal with complicated medical challenges. In most cases, specialists see cases referred by primary-care veterinarians, make diagnoses and set up management plans. From there, the animals' ongoing care is returned to their primary-care veterinarians. This important team approach to your pet's medical care needs has provided opportunities for advanced care and an unparalleled level of quality to be delivered.

With all of the opportunities for your pet to receive high-quality veterinary medical care, there is another topic that needs to be addressed at the same time—cost. It's been said that you can have excellent health-care or inexpensive healthcare, but never both; this is as true in veterinary medicine as it is in human medicine. While veterinary costs are a fraction of what the same services cost in the human healthcare arena, it is still difficult to deal with unanticipated medical costs, especially since they can easily creep into hundreds or even thousands of dollars if specialists or emergency services become involved. However, there are ways of managing these risks. The easiest is to buy pet health insurance and realize that its foremost purpose is not to cover routine health care visits but rather to serve as an umbrella for those rainy days when your pet needs medical

A once-annual tooth scaling at the vet's office proves to be critical to your Scottie's optimal dental health.

care and you don't want to worry about whether or not you can afford that care.

Pet insurance policies are very cost-effective (and very inexpensive by human health insurance standards), but make sure that you buy the policy long before you intend to use it (preferably starting in puppyhood, because coverage will exclude pre-existing conditions) and that you are actually buying an indemnity insurance plan from an insurance company that is regulated by your state. Many insurance policy look-alikes are actually discount clubs that are only redeemable at specific locations and for specific services. An indemnity plan covers your pet at almost all veterinary, specialty and emergency practices and is an excellent way to manage your pet's ongoing healthcare needs.

VACCINATIONS AND INFECTIOUS DISEASES

There has never been an easier time to prevent a variety of infectious diseases in your dog, but these advances come with a price—choice. Now, while it may seem that choice is a good thing (and it is), it has never been more difficult for the pet owner (or the veterinarian) to make an informed decision about the best way to protect

DOGGIE DENTAL DON'TS
A veterinary dental exam is necessary if you notice one or any combination of the following in your dog:
- Broken, loose or missing teeth
- Loss of appetite (which could be due to mouth pain or illness caused by infection)
- Gum abnormalities, including redness, swelling and/or bleeding
- Drooling, with or without blood
- Yellowing of the teeth and/or gumline, indicating tartar
- Bad breath.

pets through vaccination.

Years ago, it was just accepted that puppies got a starter series of vaccinations and then annual "boosters" throughout their lives to keep them protected. As more and more vaccines became available, consumers wanted the convenience of having all of that protection in a single injection. The result was "multivalent" vaccines that crammed a lot of protection into a single syringe. The manufacturers' recommendations were to give the vaccines annually, and this was a simple enough protocol to follow. However, as veterinary medicine has become more sophisticated and we have started looking more at health-care quandaries rather than convenience, it became necessary to reevaluate the situation and deal with some tough questions. It is important to realize that whether or not to use a particular vaccine depends on the risk of contracting the disease against which it protects, the severity of the disease it if is contracted, the duration of immunity provided by the vaccine, the safety of the product and the needs of the individual animal. In a very general sense, rabies,

Vitamins Recommended for Dogs

Some breeders and vets recommend the addition of vitamins to a dog's diet—others do not. Before embarking on a vitamin program, consult your vet.

Vitamin / Dosage	Food source	Benefits
A / 10,000 IU/week	Eggs, butter, yogurt, meat	Skin, eyes, hind legs, haircoat
B / Varies	Organs, cottage cheese, sardines	Appetite, fleas, heart, skin and coat
C / 2000 mg+	Fruit, legumes, leafy green vegetables	Healing, arthritis, kidneys
D / Varies	Cod liver, cheese, organs, eggs	Bones, teeth, endocrine system
E / 250 IU daily	Leafy green vegetables, meat, wheat germ oil	Skin, muscles, nerves, healing, digestion
F / Varies	Fish oils, raw meat	Heart, skin, coat, fleas
K / Varies	Naturally in body, not through food	Blood clotting

Don't Eat the Daisies!

Many plants and flowers are beautiful to look at but can be highly toxic if ingested by your dog. Reactions range from abdominal pain and vomiting to convulsions and death. If the following plants are in your home, remove them. If they are outside your house or in your garden, avoid accidents by making sure your dog is never left unsupervised in those locations.

Azalea
Belladonna
Bird of Paradise
Bulbs
Calla lily
Cardinal flower
Castor bean
Chinaberry tree
Daphne

Dumb cane
Dutchman's breeches
Elephant's ear
Hydrangea
Jack-in-the-pulpit
Jasmine
Jimsonweed
Larkspur
Laurel
Lily of the valley

Mescal bean
Mushrooms
Nightshade
Philodendron
Poinsettia
Prunus species
Tobacco
Yellow jasmine
Yews, *Taxus* species

distemper, hepatitis and parvovirus are considered core vaccine needs, while parainfluenza, *Bordetella bronchiseptica,* leptospirosis, coronavirus and borreliosis (Lyme disease) are considered non-core needs and best reserved for animals that demonstrate reasonable risk of contracting the diseases.

THE GREAT VACCINATION DEBATE

What kinds of questions need to be addressed? When the vet injects multiple organisms at the same time, might some of the components interfere with one another in the development of immunologic protection? We don't have the comprehensive answer to that question, but it does appear that the immune system better handles agents when given individually. Unfortunately, most manufacturers still bundle their vaccine components because that is what most pet owners want, so getting vaccines with single components can sometimes be difficult.

Another question has to do with how often vaccines should be given. Again, this seems to be different for each vaccine component. There seems to be

BEWARE THE SPIDER

Should you worry about a spider spinning its poisonous web over your dog? Like other venomous critters, spiders can bite dogs and cause severe reactions. The most deleterious eight-leggers are the black and red widow spiders, brown recluse and common brown spiders, whose bites can cause local pain, cramping, spasms and restlessness. It is these signals that tell owners there is a problem, as the bites themselves can be difficult to locate under your dog's coat. Another vicious arachnid is the bark scorpion, whose bite can cause excessive drooling, tearing, urination and defecation. Often spider and scorpion bites are misdiagnosed because vets don't recognize the signs and owners didn't witness the escape of the avenging arachnid.

general consensus that a puppy (or a dog with an unknown vaccination history) should get a series of vaccinations to initially stimulate his immunity and then a booster at one year of age, but, after that, even the veterinary associations and colleges have trouble reaching agreement. Rabies vaccination schedules are not debated, because vaccine schedules for this contagious and devastating disease are determined by government agencies. Regarding the rest, some recommend that

we continue to give the vaccines annually because this method has worked well as a disease preventive for decades and delivers predictable protection. Others recommend that some of the vaccines only need to be given every second or third year, as this can be done without affecting levels of protection. This is probably true for some vaccine components (such as hepatitis), but there have been no large studies to demonstrate what the optimal interval should be and whether the same principles hold true for all breeds.

It may be best to just measure titers, which are protective blood levels of various vaccine components, on an annual basis, but that too is not without controversy. Scientists have not precisely determined the minimum titer of specific vaccine components that will be guaranteed to provide a pet with protection. Pets with very high titers will clearly be protected and those with very low titers will need repeat vaccinations, but there is also a large "gray zone" of pets that probably have intermediate protection and may or may not need repeat vaccination, depending on their risk of coming into contact with the disease.

These questions leave primary-care veterinarians in a very uncomfortable position,

THE **ABC**S OF
Emergency Care

Abrasions
Clean wound with running water or 3% hydrogen peroxide. Pat dry with gauze and spray with antibiotic. Do not cover.

Animal Bites
Clean area with soap and saline or water. Apply pressure to any bleeding area. Apply antibiotic ointment.

Antifreeze Poisoning
Induce vomiting and take dog to the vet.

Bee Sting
Remove stinger and apply soothing lotion or cold compress; give antihistamine in proper dosage.

Bleeding
Apply pressure directly to wound with gauze or towel for five to ten minutes. If wound does not stop bleeding, wrap wound with gauze and adhesive tape.

Bloat/Gastric Torsion
Immediately take the dog to the vet or emergency clinic; phone from car. No time to waste.

Burns
Chemical: Bathe dog with water and pet shampoo. Rinse in saline. Apply antibiotic ointment.

Acid: Rinse with water. Apply one part baking soda, two parts water to affected area.

Alkali: Rinse with water. Apply one part vinegar, four parts water to affected area.

Electrical: Apply antibiotic ointment. Seek veterinary assistance immediately.

Choking
If the dog is on the verge of collapsing, wedge a solid object, such as the handle of screwdriver, between molars on one side of mouth to keep mouth open. Pull tongue out. Use long-nosed pliers or fingers to remove foreign object. Do not push the object down the dog's throat. For small or medium dogs, hold dog upside down by hind legs and shake firmly to dislodge foreign object.

Chlorine Ingestion
With clean water, rinse the mouth and eyes. Give dog water to drink; contact the vet.

Constipation
Feed dog 2 tablespoons bran flakes with each meal. Encourage drinking water. Mix 1/4 teaspoon mineral oil in dog's food.

Diarrhea
Withhold food for 12 to 24 hours. Feed dog anti-diarrheal with eyedropper. When feeding resumes, feed one part boiled hamburger, one part plain cooked rice, 1/4- to 3/4-cup four times daily.

Dog Bite
Snip away hair around puncture wound; clean with 3% hydrogen peroxide; apply tincture of iodine. If wound appears deep, take the dog to the vet.

Frostbite
Wrap the dog in a heavy blanket. Warm affected area with a warm bath for ten minutes. Red color to skin will return with circulation; if tissues are pale after 20 minutes, contact the vet.

Heat Stroke
Submerge the dog in cold water; if no response within ten minutes, contact the vet.

Hot Spots
Mix 2 packets Domeboro® with 2 cups water. Saturate cloth with mixture and apply to hot spots for 15-30 minutes. Apply antibiotic ointment. Repeat every six to eight hours.

Poisonous Plants
Wash affected area with soap and water. Cleanse with alcohol. For foxtail/grass, apply antibiotic ointment.

Rat Poison Ingestion
Induce vomiting. Keep dog calm, maintain dog's normal body temperature (use blanket or heating pad). Get to the vet for antidote.

Shock
Keep the dog calm and warm; call for veterinary assistance.

Snake Bite
If possible, bandage the area and apply pressure. If the area is not conducive to bandaging, use ice to control bleeding. Get immediate help from the vet.

Tick Removal
Apply flea and tick spray directly on tick. Wait one minute. Using tweezers or wearing plastic gloves, grasp the tick's body firmly. Apply antibiotic ointment.

Vomiting
Restrict dog's water intake; offer a few ice cubes. Withhold food for next meal. Contact vet if vomiting persists longer than 24 hours.

one that is not easy to resolve. Do they recommend annual vaccination in a manner that has demonstrated successful protection for decades, do they recommend skipping vaccines some years and hope that the protection lasts or do they measure blood tests (titers) and hope that the results are convincing enough to clearly indicate whether repeat vaccination is warranted?

These aren't the only vaccination questions impacting pets, owners and veterinarians. Other controversies focus on whether vaccines should be dosed according to body weight (currently they are administered in uniform doses, regardless of the animal's size), whether there are breed-specific issues important in determining vaccination programs (for instance, we know that some breeds have a harder time mounting an appropriate immune response to parvovirus vaccine and might benefit from a different dose or injection interval) and which type of vaccine—live-virus or inactivated—offers more advantages with fewer disadvantages. Clearly, there are many more questions than there are answers. The important thing, as a pet owner, is to be aware of the issues and be able to work with your veterinarian to make

decisions that are right for your pet. Be an informed consumer and you will appreciate the deliberation required in tailoring a vaccination program to best meet the needs of your pet. Expect also that this is an ongoing, ever-changing topic of debate; thus the decisions you make this year won't necessarily be the same as the ones you make next year.

COMMON VACCINATIONS
Now that you are more confused than ever about vaccination, it is a good time to discuss some of the diseases that create the need for vaccination in the first place. Following are the major canine infectious diseases and a simple explanation of each.

Rabies is a devastating viral disease that can be fatal in dogs and people. In fact, vaccination of dogs and cats is an important public-health measure to create a resistant animal buffer population to protect people from contracting the disease. Vaccination schedules are determined on a government level and are not optional for pet owners; rabies vaccination is required by law in all 50 states.

Parvovirus is a severe, potentially life-threatening disease that is easily transmitted between dogs. There are four strains of the virus, but it is believed that there is significant

BEER SUDS TO FOAMING DOGS: PASTEUR TO THE RESCUE

Rabies, as old as any plague, dates back to Babylonian days, the 23rd century BC. The term may derive from the Sanskrit word "rabhas," which translates "to do violence." In the 16th century, Girolama Fracastoro was the first scientist to describe the disease, which he did some 350 years prior to Louis Pasteur, the scientist well known in his day for "pasteurizing" milk and beer.

In the 1870s, Pasteur emerged as a much-needed savior from terror in an irrational world. Ironically, his first effort in dealing with human disease was a vaccine for anthrax, which, like rabies, affects humans and animals alike. Rabies scourged Europe with a vengeance, and victims of the "violent virus" were either killed or committed suicide. Pasteur developed a vaccine for rabies by injecting brain material from a rabid dog into the bloodstream of a healthy dog. Once he developed a way of adjusting the virulence of the inoculation, he could build up the animal's resistance to the disease through a series of stronger inoculations. Since the virus developed slowly in an affected dog, the dog was able to develop immunity to the rabies before the incubation period had ended. After much experimentation, Pasteur was able to treat humans and, in 1885, his remarkable vaccination saved the first of millions of human beings.

"cross-protection" between strains that may be included in individual vaccines.

Distemper is another potentially severe and life-threatening disease with a relatively high risk of exposure, especially in certain regions. In very high-risk distemper environments, young pups may be vaccinated with human measles vaccine, a related virus that offers cross-protection when administered at 4-10 weeks of age.

Hepatitis is caused by canine adenovirus type 1 (CAV-1), but since vaccination with the causative virus has a higher rate of adverse effects, cross-protection is derived from the use of adenovirus type 2 (CAV-2), a cause of respiratory disease and one of the potential causes of canine cough. Vaccination with CAV-2 provides long-term immunity against hepatitis but relatively less protection against respiratory infection.

Canine cough (tracheobronchitis) is actually a fairly complicated result of viral and bacterial offenders; therefore, even with vaccination, protection is incomplete. Wherever dogs congregate, canine cough will likely be spread among them. Intranasal vaccination with *Bordetella* and parainfluenza is the best safeguard, but the duration of immunity does not appear to be very long, typically a year at most. These are non-core vaccines, but vaccination is sometimes mandated by boarding kennels, obedience classes, dog shows and other places where dogs congregate to try to minimize spread of infection.

Leptospirosis is a potentially fatal disease that is more common in some geographic regions. It is capable of being spread to humans. The disease varies with the individual "serovar," or strain, of *Leptospira* involved; since there does not appear to be much cross-protection between serovars, protection is only as good as the likelihood that the serovar in the vaccine is the same as the one in the pet's local environment. Problems with *Leptospira* vaccines are that protection does not last very long, side effects are not uncommon and a large percentage of dogs (perhaps 30%) may not respond to vaccination.

Borrelia burgdorferi is the cause of **Lyme disease,** the risk of which varies with the geographic area in which the pet lives and travels. Lyme disease is spread by deer ticks in the eastern US and western black-legged ticks in the western part of the country, and the risk of exposure is high in some regions. Lameness, fever and inappetence are most commonly seen in affected dogs. The extent of protection from the vaccine has not been conclusively demonstrated.

Coronavirus has a high risk of exposure, especially in areas where dogs congregate, but it typically causes only mild to moderate digestive upset (diarrhea, vomiting, etc.). Vaccines are available, but the duration of protection is believed to be relatively short and the effectiveness of the vaccine in preventing infection is considered low.

There are many other vaccinations available, including those for Giardia and canine adenovirus-1. While there may be some specific indications for their use, and local risk factors to be considered, they are not widely recommended for most dogs.

NEUTERING/SPAYING

Sterilization procedures (neutering for males/spaying for females) are meant to accomplish several purposes. While the underlying premise is to address the risk of pet overpopulation, there are also some medical and behavioral benefits to the surgeries as well. For females, spaying prior to the first estrus (heat cycle) leads to a marked reduction in the risk

SPAY'S THE WAY

Although spaying a female dog qualifies as major surgery—an ovariohysterectomy, in fact—this procedure is regarded as routine when performed by a qualified veterinarian on a healthy dog. The advantages to spaying a bitch are many and great. Spayed dogs do not develop uterine cancer or any life-threatening diseases of the genitals. Likewise, spayed dogs are at a significantly reduced risk for breast cancer. Bitches (and owners) are relieved of the demands of heat cycles. A spayed bitch will not leave bloody stains on your furniture during estrus, and you will not have to contend with single-minded macho males trying to climb your fence in order to seduce your bitch. The spayed bitch's coat will not show the ill effects of her estrogen level's climbing such as a dull, lackluster outer coat or patches of hairlessness.

of mammary cancer. There are also no manifestations of "heat" to attract male dogs nor bleeding in the house. For males, neutering prevents testicular cancer and reduces the risk of prostate problems. There may be some limited reduction in aggressive behaviors toward other dogs and (as sex-appropriate) some diminishing of urine marking, roaming and mounting.

While neutering and spaying do indeed prevent animals from contributing to pet overpopulation, even no-cost and low-cost neutering options have not eliminated the problem. Perhaps one of the main reasons for this is that individuals who intentionally breed their dogs and those who allow their animals to run at large are the main causes of unwanted offspring. Also, animals in shelters are often there because they were abandoned or relinquished, not because they came from unplanned matings. Neutering/spaying is important, but it should be considered in the context of the real causes of animals' ending up in shelters and eventually being euthanized.

One of the important considerations regarding sterilization is that it is a surgical procedure. This sometimes gets lost in discussions of low-cost procedures and commoditization of the process. In females, spaying is specifically referred to as an ovariohysterectomy. In this procedure, a midline incision is made in the abdomen and the entire uterus and both ovaries are surgically removed. While this is a major invasive surgical procedure, it usually has few complications, because it is typically performed on healthy young animals. However, it is a major surgery, as any woman who has had a

surgery. In addition, there is now a chemical sterilization option in which a solution is injected into each testicle, leading to atrophy of the sperm-producing cells. This can typically be done under sedation rather than full anesthesia. This is a relatively new approach, and there are no long-term clinical studies yet available.

Neutering/spaying is typically done around six months of age at most veterinary hospitals, although techniques have been pioneered to perform the procedures in animals as young as eight weeks of age. In general, the surgeries on the very young animals are done for the specific reason of sterilizing them before they go to their new homes. This is done in some shelter hospitals for assurance that the animals will definitely not produce any pups. Otherwise, these organizations need to rely on owners to comply with their wishes to have the animals "altered" at a later date, something that does not always happen.

There are some exciting immunocontraceptive "vaccines" currently under development, and there may be a time when contraception in pets will not require surgical procedures. We anxiously await these developments.

Most breeders agree that neutering/spaying grants pure-bred dogs longer, healthier lives.

hysterectomy will attest.

In males, neutering has traditionally referred to castration, which involves the surgical removal of both testicles. While still a significant piece of surgery, there is not the abdominal exposure that is required in the female

Recognizing a Sick Dog

Unlike colicky babies and cranky children, our canine kids cannot tell us when they are feeling ill. Therefore, there are a number of signs that owners can identify to know that their dogs are not feeling well.

**Take note of
physical manifestations such as:**

- unusual bad odor, including bad breath
- excessive shedding
- wax in the ears, chronic ear irritation
- oily, flaky, dull haircoat
- mucus, tearing or similar discharge in the eyes
- fleas or mites
- mucus in stool, diarrhea
- sensitivity to petting or handling
- licking at paws, scratching face, etc.

**Keep an eye out for
behavioral changes as well including:**

- lethargy, idleness
- lack of patience or general irritability
- lack of interest in food
- phobias (fear of people, loud noises, etc.)
- strange behavior, suspicion, fear
- coprophagia
- more frequent barking
- whimpering, crying

Get Well Soon

You don't need a DVM to provide good TLC to your sick or recovering dog, but you do need to pay attention to some details that normally wouldn't bother him. The following tips will aid Fido's recovery and get him back on his paws again:

- Keep his space free of irritating smells, like heavy perfumes and air fresheners.
- Rest is the best medicine! Avoid harsh lighting that will prevent your dog from sleeping. Shade him from bright sunlight during the day and dim the lights in the evening.
- Keep the noise level down. Animals are more sensitive to sound when they are sick.

- Be attentive to any necessary temperature adjustments. A dog with a fever needs a cool room and cold liquids. A bitch that is whelping or recovering from surgery will be more comfortable in a warm room, consuming warm liquids and food.
- You wouldn't send a sick child back to school early, so don't rush your dog back into a full routine until he seems absolutely ready.

S.E.M. BY DR. DENNIS KUNKEL, UNIVERSITY OF HAWAII

A scanning electron micrograph of a dog flea, *Ctenocephalides canis*, on dog hair.

EXTERNAL PARASITES

FLEAS

Fleas have been around for millions of years and, while we have better tools now for controlling them than at any time in the past, there still is little chance that they will end up on an endangered species list. Actually, they are very well adapted to living on our pets, and they continue to adapt as we make advances.

The female flea can consume 15 times her weight in blood during active reproduction and can lay as many as 40 eggs a day. These eggs are very resistant to the effects of insecticides. They hatch into larvae, which then mature and spin cocoons. The immature fleas reside in this pupal stage until the time is right for feeding. This pupal stage is also very resistant to the effects of insecticides, and pupae can last in the environment without feeding for many months. Newly emergent fleas are attracted to animals by the warmth of the animals' bodies, movement and exhaled carbon dioxide. However, when they first emerge from their cocoons, they orient towards light; thus, when an animal passes between a flea and the light source, casting a shadow, the flea pounces and starts to feed. If the animal turns out to be a dog or cat, the reproductive cycle continues. If the flea lands on another type of animal, including a person, the flea will bite but will then look for a more appropriate host. An emerging adult flea can survive without feeding for up to 12 months but, once it tastes blood, it can only survive off its host for 3 to 4 days.

It was once thought that fleas spend most of their lives in the environment, but we now know that fleas won't willingly jump off a dog unless leaping to another dog or when physically removed by brushing, bathing or other manipulation. Flea eggs, on the other hand, are shiny and smooth, and they roll off the animal and into the environment. The eggs, larvae and pupae then exist in the environment, but once the adult finds a susceptible animal, it's home sweet home until the flea is convinced to seek refuge elsewhere.

Since adult fleas live on the animal and immature forms survive in the environment, a successful treatment plan must address all stages of the flea life cycle. There are now several safe and effective flea-control products that can be applied on a monthly

> ## FLEA PREVENTION FOR YOUR DOG
> - Discuss with your veterinarian the safest product to protect your dog, likely in the form of a monthly tablet or a liquid preparation placed on the back of the dog's neck.
> - For dogs suffering from flea-bite dermatitis, a shampoo or topical insecticide treatment is required.
> - Your lawn and property should be sprayed with an insecticide designed to kill fleas and ticks that lurk outdoors.
> - Using a flea comb, check the dog's coat regularly for any signs of parasites.
> - Practice good housekeeping: vacuum floors, carpets and furniture regularly, especially in the areas that the dog frequents, and wash the dog's bedding weekly.
> - Follow up house-cleaning with carpet shampoos and sprays to rid the house of fleas at all stages of development. Insect growth regulators are the safest option.

basis. These include fipronil, imidacloprid, selamectin and permethrin (found in several formulations). Most of these products have significant flea-killing rates within 24 hours. However, none of them will control the immature forms in the environment. To accomplish this, there are a variety of insect growth regulators that can be

THE FLEA'S LIFE CYCLE

What came first, the flea or the egg? This age-old mystery is more difficult to comprehend than the actual cycle of the flea. Fleas usually live only about four months. A female can lay 2,000 eggs in her lifetime.

Egg

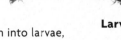

Larva

After ten days of rolling around your carpet or under your furniture, the eggs hatch into larvae, which feed on various and sundry debris. In days or months, depending on the climate, the larvae spin a cocoon and develop into the pupal or nymph stage, which quickly develop into fleas.

Pupa

These immature fleas must locate a host within 10 to 14 days or they will die. Only about 1% of the flea population exist as adult fleas, while the other 99% exist as eggs, larvae or pupae.

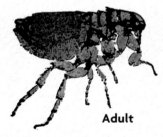

Adult

KILL FLEAS THE NATURAL WAY

If you choose not to go the route of conventional medication, there are some natural ways to ward off fleas:

- Dust your dog with a natural flea powder, comprised of such herbal goodies as rosemary, wormwood, pennyroyal, citronella, rue, tobacco powder and eucalyptus.
- Apply diatomaceous earth, the fossilized remains of single-cell algae, to your carpets, furniture and pet's bedding. Even though it's not good for dogs, it's even worse for fleas, which will dry up swiftly and die.
- Brush your dog frequently, give him adequate exercise and let him fast occasionally. All of these activities strengthen the dog's system and make him more resistant to disease and parasites.
- Bathe your dog with a capful of pennyroyal or eucalyptus oil.
- Feed a natural diet, free of additives and preservatives. Add some fresh garlic and brewer's yeast to the dog's morning portion, as these have flea-repelling properties.

sprayed into the environment (e.g., pyriproxyfen, methoprene, fenoxycarb) as well as insect development inhibitors such as lufenuron that can be administered. These compounds have no effect on adult fleas, but they stop immature forms from developing

into adults. In years gone by, we relied heavily on toxic insecticides (such as organophosphates, organochlorines and carbamates) to manage the flea problem, but today's options are not only much safer to use on our pets but also safer for the environment.

TICKS

Ticks are members of the spider group (arachnids) and are blood-sucking parasites capable of transmitting a variety of diseases, including Lyme disease, ehrlichiosis, babesiosis and Rocky Mountain spotted fever. It's easy to see ticks on your own skin, but it is more of a challenge when your furry companion is affected. Whenever you happen to be planning a stroll in a tick-infested area (especially forests, grassy or wooded areas or parks) be prepared to do a thorough inspection of your dog afterward to search for ticks. Ticks can be tricky, so make sure you spend time looking in the ears, between the toes and everywhere else where a tick might hide. Ticks need to be attached for 24–72 hours before they transmit most of the diseases that they carry, so you do have a window of opportunity for some preventative intervention.

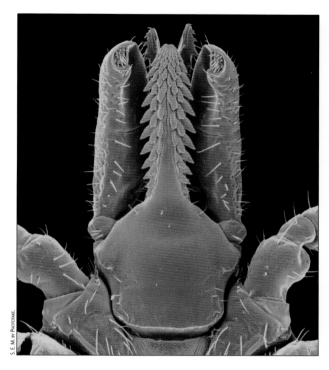

S. E. M. BY PHOTOTAKE.

A scanning electron micrograph of the head of a female deer tick, *Ixodes dammini,* a parasitic tick that carries Lyme disease.

A TICKING BOMB

There is nothing good about a tick's harpooning his nose into your dog's skin. Among the diseases caused by ticks are Rocky Mountain spotted fever, canine ehrlichiosis, canine babesiosis, canine hepatozoonosis and Lyme disease. If a dog is allergic to the saliva of a female wood tick, he can develop tick paralysis.

Female ticks live to eat and breed. They can lay between 4,000 and 5,000 eggs and they die soon after. Males, on the other hand, live only to mate with other females and continue the process as long as they are able. Most ticks live on multiple hosts before parasitizing dogs. The immature forms typically reside on grass and shrubs, waiting for suscep-tible animals to walk by. The larvae and nymph stages typically feed on wildlife.

If only a few ticks are present on a dog, they can be plucked out, but it is important to remove the entire head and mouthparts,

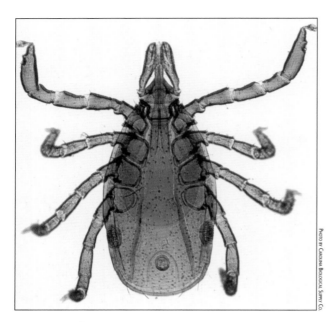

PHOTO BY CAROLINA BIOLOGICAL SUPPLY CO.

Deer tick,
Ixodes dammini.

disposed of in a container of alcohol or flushed down the toilet.

Some of the newer flea products, specifically those with fipronil, selamectin and permethrin, have effect against some, but not all, species of tick. Flea collars containing appropriate insecticides (e.g., propoxur, chlorfenvinphos) can aid in tick control. In most areas, such collars should be placed on animals in March, at the beginning of the tick season, and changed regularly. Leaving the collar on when the insecticide level is waning invites the development of resistance. Amitraz collars are also good for tick control, and the active ingredient does not interfere with other flea-control products. The ingredient helps prevent the attachment of ticks to the skin and will cause those ticks already on the skin to detach themselves.

which may be deeply embedded in the skin. This is best accomplished with forceps designed especially for this purpose; fingers can be used, but should be protected with rubber gloves, plastic wrap or at least a paper towel. The tick should be grasped as closely as possible to the animal's skin and should be pulled upward with steady, even pressure. Do not squeeze, crush or puncture the body of the tick or you risk exposure to any disease carried by that tick. Once the ticks have been removed, the sites of attachment should be disinfected. Your hands should then be washed with soap and water to further minimize risk of contagion. The tick should be

TICK CONTROL

Removal of underbrush and leaf litter and the thinning of trees in areas where tick control is desired are recommended. These actions remove the cover and food sources for small animals that serve as hosts for ticks. With continued mowing of grasses in these areas, the probability of ticks' surviving is further reduced. A variety of insecticide ingredients (e.g., resmethrin, carbaryl, permethrin, chlorpyrifos, dioxathion and allethrin) are registered for tick control around the home.

MITES

Mites are tiny arachnid parasites that parasitize the skin of dogs. Skin diseases caused by mites are referred to as "mange," and there are many different forms seen in dogs. These forms are very different from one another, each one warranting an individual description.

Sarcoptic mange, or scabies, is one of the itchiest conditions that affects dogs. The microscopic *Sarcoptes* mites burrow into the superficial layers of the skin and can drive dogs crazy with itchiness. They are also communicable to people, although they can't complete their reproductive cycle on people. Not only are the mites tiny but also are often difficult to find when trying to make a diagnosis. Skin scrapings from multiple areas are examined microscopically but, even then, sometimes the mites cannot be found.

Fortunately, scabies is relatively easy to treat, and there are a variety of products that will successfully kill the mites. Since the mites can't live in the environment for very long without feeding, a complete cure is usually possible within four to eight weeks.

Cheyletiellosis is caused by a relatively large mite, which sometimes can be seen even without a microscope. Often referred to as "walking dandruff," this also causes itching, but not usually as profound as with scabies.

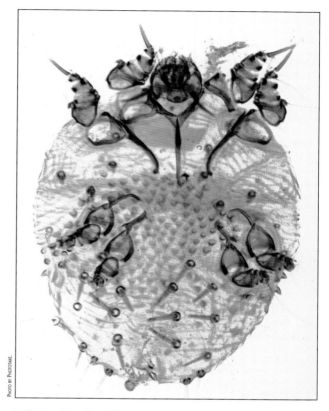

PHOTO BY PHOTOTAKE.

Sarcoptes scabiei, commonly known as the "itch mite."

While *Cheyletiella* mites can survive somewhat longer in the environment than scabies mites, they too are relatively easy to treat, being responsive not only to the medications used to treat scabies but also often to flea-control products.

Otodectes cynotis is the cause of ear mites and is one of the more common causes of mange, especially in young dogs in shelters or pet stores. That's because the mites are typically present in large numbers and are quickly spread to

Micrograph of a dog louse, *Heterodoxus spiniger.* Female lice attach their eggs to the hairs of the dog. As the eggs hatch, the larval lice bite and feed on the blood. Lice can also feed on dead skin and hair. This feeding activity can cause hair loss and skin problems.

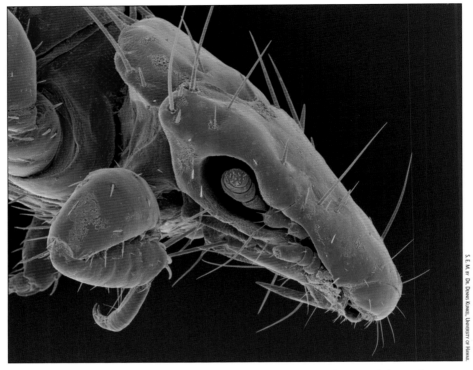

S. E. M. BY DR. DENNIS KUNKEL, UNIVERSITY OF HAWAII.

nearby animals. The mites rarely do much harm, but can be difficult to eradicate if the treatment regimen is not comprehensive. While many try to treat the condition with ear drops only, this is the most common cause of treatment failure. Ear drops cause the mites to simply move out of the ears and as far away as possible (usually to the base of the tail) until the insecticide levels in the ears drop to an acceptable level—then it's back to business as usual! The successful treatment of ear mites requires treating all animals in the household with a systemic insecticide, such as selamectin, or a combination of miticidal ear drops combined with whole-body flea-control preparations.

Demodicosis, sometimes referred to as red mange, can be one of the most difficult forms of mange to treat. Part of the problem has to do with the fact that the mites live in the hair follicles, so are relatively well shielded from topical and systemic products. The main issue, however, is that demodectic mange typically only results when there is some underlying process interfering with the dog's immune system.

Since *Demodex* mites are normal residents of the skin of

mammals, including humans, there is usually only a mite population explosion when the immune system fails to keep the number of mites in check. In young animals, the immune deficit may be transient or it may reflect an actual inherited immune problem. In older animals, demodicosis is usually seen only when there is another disease hampering the immune system, such as diabetes, cancer, thyroid problems or the use of immune-suppressing drugs. Accordingly, treatment involves not only trying to kill the mange mites but also discerning what is interfering with immune function and correcting it if possible.

Chiggers represent several different species of mite that don't parasitize dogs specifically, but do latch on to passersby and can cause irritation. The problem is most prevalent in wooded areas in the late summer and fall. Treatment is not difficult, as the mites do not complete their life cycle on dogs and are susceptible to a variety of insecticides.

MOSQUITOES

Mosquitoes have long been known to transmit a variety of diseases to people, as well as just being biting pests during warm weather. They also pose a real risk to pets. Not only do they carry deadly heartworms but recently there also has been much concern over their involvement with West Nile virus. While we can avoid heartworm with the use of preventative medications, there are no such preventatives for West Nile virus. The only method of prevention in endemic areas is active mosquito control. Fortunately, most dogs that have been exposed to the virus only developed flu-like symptoms and, to date, there have not been the large number of reported deaths in canines as seen in some other species.

Illustration of *Demodex folliculoram.*

ILLUSTRATION BY PHOTOTAKE.

MOSQUITO REPELLENT

Low concentrations of DEET (less than 10%), found in many human mosquito repellents, have been safely used in dogs but, in these concentrations, probably only give about two hours of protection. DEET may be safe in these small concentrations, but since it is not licensed for use on dogs, there is no research proving its safety for dogs. Products containing permethrin give the longest-lasting protection, perhaps two to four weeks. As DEET is not licensed for use on dogs, and both DEET and permethrin can be quite toxic to cats, appropriate care should be exercised. Other products, such as those containing oil of citronella, also have some mosquito-repellent activity, but typically have relatively short duration of action.

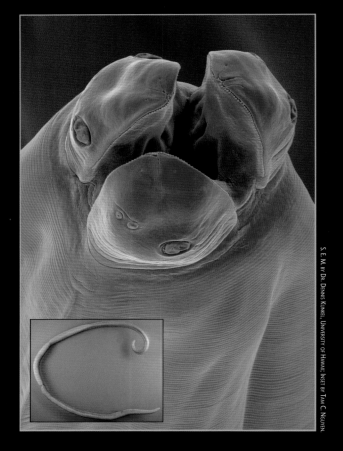

S. E. M. BY DR. DENNIS KUNKEL, UNIVERSITY OF HAWAII. INSET BY TAM C. NGUYEN.

Roundworm, *Toxocara canis*, showing the mouth with three lips. Inset: Photomicrograph of a roundworm, *Ascaris lumbricoides*.

INTERNAL PARASITES

ROUNDWORMS

Roundworms are intestinal parasites that rarely cause severe disease in dogs. Nonetheless, they are of major public health significance because they can be transferred to people. Sadly, it is children who are most commonly affected with the parasite, probably from inadvertently ingesting roundworm-contaminated soil. In fact, many yards and children's sandboxes contain appreciable numbers of roundworm eggs. So while roundworms don't bite dogs or latch on to their intestines to suck blood, they do cause some nasty medical conditions in children and are best eradicated from our furry friends. Because pups can start passing roundworm eggs by three weeks of age, most parasite-control programs begin at two weeks of age and are repeated every two weeks until pups are eight weeks old. It is important to

HOOKED ON ANCYLOSTOMA

Adult dogs can become infected by the bloodsucking nematodes we commonly call hookworms via ingesting larvae from the ground or via the larvae penetrating the dog's skin. It is not uncommon for infected dogs to show no symptoms of hookworm infestation. Sometimes, symptoms occur within ten days of exposure. These symptoms can include bloody diarrhea, anemia, loss of weight and general weakness. Dogs pass the hookworm eggs in their stools, which serves as the vet's method of identifying the infestation. The hookworm larvae can encyst themselves in the dog's tissues and be released when the dog is experiencing stress.

Caused by *Ancylostoma braziliense*, whose common host is the dog, cutaneous larva migrans, affects humans, causing itching and lumps and streaks beneath the surface of the skin.

S. E. M. BY DR. DENNIS KUNKEL, UNIVERSITY OF HAWAII.

realize that bitches can pass roundworms to their pups even if they test negative prior to whelping. Accordingly, bitches are best treated at the same time as the pups.

HOOKWORMS

Unlike roundworms, hookworms do latch on to a dog's intestinal tract and can cause significant loss of blood and protein. Similar to roundworms, hookworms can be transmitted to humans, where they cause a condition known as cutaneous larva migrans. Dogs can become infected either by consuming the infective larvae or by the larvae's penetrating the skin directly. People most often get infected when they are lying on the ground (such as on a beach) and the larvae penetrate the skin. Yes, the larvae can penetrate through a beach blanket. Hookworms are typically susceptible to the same medications used to treat roundworms.

Hookworm, *Ancylostoma caninum*, a small parasitic worm about 1 mm in length at full size. Inset: Posterior end of a male hookworm.

WHIPWORMS

Whipworms latch on to the lower aspects of the dog's colon and can cause cramping and diarrhea. Eggs do not start to appear in the dog's feces until about three months after the dog was infected. This worm has a peculiar life cycle, which makes it more difficult to control than roundworms or hookworms. The good thing is that whipworms rarely are transferred to people.

Some of the medications used to treat roundworms and hookworms are also effective against whipworms, but, in general, a separate treatment protocol is needed. Since most of the medications are effective against the adults but not the eggs or larvae, treatment is typically repeated in three weeks,

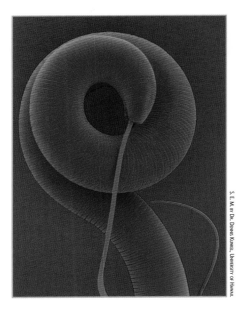

Adult whipworm, *Trichuris* sp., an intestinal parasite.

S. E. M. BY DR. DENNIS KUNKEL, UNIVERSITY OF HAWAII

WORM-CONTROL GUIDELINES
- Practice sanitary habits with your dog and home.
- Clean up after your dog and don't let him sniff or eat other dogs' droppings.
- Control insects and fleas in the dog's environment. Fleas, lice, cockroaches, beetles, mice and rats can act as hosts for various worms.
- Prevent dogs from eating uncooked meat, raw poultry and dead animals.
- Keep dogs and children from playing in sand and soil.
- Kennel dogs on cement or gravel; avoid dirt runs.
- Administer heartworm preventatives regularly.
- Have your vet examine your dog's stools at your annual visits.
- Select a boarding kennel carefully, so as to avoid contamination from other dogs or an unsanitary environment.
- Prevent dogs from roaming. Obey local leash laws.

and then often in three months as well. Unfortunately, since dogs don't develop resistance to whipworms, it is difficult to prevent them from getting reinfected if they visit soil contaminated with whipworm eggs.

TAPEWORMS

There are many different species of tapeworm that affect dogs, but *Dipylidium caninum* is probably the most common and is spread by fleas. Flea larvae feed on organic debris and tapeworm eggs in the environment and, when a dog chews at himself and manages to ingest fleas, he might get a dose of tapeworm at the same time. The tapeworm then develops further in the intestine of the dog.

The tapeworm itself, which latches on to the intestinal wall, is composed of numerous segments. When the segments break off into the intestine (as proglottids), they may accumulate around the rectum, like grains of rice. While this tapeworm is disgusting in its behavior, it is not directly communicable to humans (although humans can also get infected by swallowing fleas).

A much more dangerous tapeworm is *Echinococcus multilocularis*, which is typically found in foxes, coyotes and wolves. The eggs are passed in the feces and infect rodents, and, when dogs eat the rodents, the dogs can be infected by thousands of adult tapeworms. While the parasites don't cause many problems in dogs, this is considered the most lethal worm infection that people can get. Take appropriate precautions if you live in an area in which these tapeworms are found. Do not use mulch that may contain feces of dogs, cats or wildlife, and discourage your pets from hunting

wildlife. Treat these tapeworm infections aggressively in pets, because if humans get infected, approximately half die.

HEARTWORMS

Heartworm disease is caused by the parasite *Dirofilaria immitis* and is seen in dogs around the world. The parasite itself, an actual worm, is spread between dogs by the bite of an infected mosquito. The mosquito injects infective larvae into the dog's skin with its bite, and these larvae develop under the skin for a period of time before making their way to the heart. There, they develop into adults, which grow and create blockage of the heart, lungs and major blood vessels there. They also start

Dog tapeworm proglottid (body segment).

Dog tapeworm, *Taenia pisiformis*.

S. E. M. BY DR. DENNIS KUNKEL, UNIVERSITY OF HAWAII

A Look at Internal Parasites

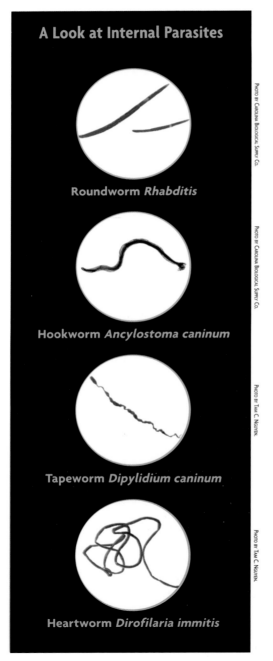

Roundworm *Rhabditis*

Hookworm *Ancylostoma caninum*

Tapeworm *Dipylidium caninum*

Heartworm *Dirofilaria immitis*

PHOTO BY CAROLINA BIOLOGICAL SUPPLY CO.

PHOTO BY CAROLINA BIOLOGICAL SUPPLY CO.

PHOTO BY TAM C. NGUYEN.

PHOTO BY TAM C. NGUYEN.

producing offspring (microfilariae) and these microfilariae circulate in the bloodstream, waiting to hitch a ride when the next mosquito bites. Once in the mosquito, the microfilariae develop into infective larvae and the entire process is repeated.

When dogs get infected with heartworm, over time they tend to develop symptoms associated with heart disease, such as coughing, exercise intolerance and potentially many other manifestations. Diagnosis is confirmed by either seeing the microfilariae themselves in blood samples or using immunologic tests (antigen testing) to identify the presence of adult heartworms. Since antigen tests measure the presence of adult heartworms, and microfilarial tests measure offspring produced by adults, neither are positive until six to seven months after the initial infection. However, the beginning of damage can occur by fifth-stage larvae as early as three months after infection. Thus, it is possible for dogs to be harboring problem-causing larvae for up to three months before either type of test would identify an infection.

The good news is that there are great protocols available for preventing heartworm in dogs. Testing is critical in the process, and it is important to understand the benefits as well as the limitations of such testing. All dogs six months of age or older that have not been on continuous heartworm preventative

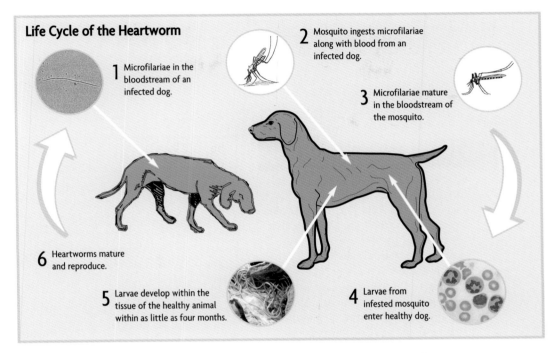

Life Cycle of the Heartworm

1 Microfilariae in the bloodstream of an infected dog.

2 Mosquito ingests microfilariae along with blood from an infected dog.

3 Microfilariae mature in the bloodstream of the mosquito.

6 Heartworms mature and reproduce.

5 Larvae develop within the tissue of the healthy animal within as little as four months.

4 Larvae from infested mosquito enter healthy dog.

medication should be screened with microfilarial or antigen tests. For dogs receiving preventative medication, periodic antigen testing helps assess the effectiveness of the preventives. The American Heartworm Society guidelines suggest that annual retesting may not be necessary when owners have absolutely provided continuous heartworm prevention. Retesting on a two- to three-year interval may be sufficient in these cases. However, your veterinarian will likely have specific guidelines under which heartworm preventatives will be prescribed, and many prefer to err on the side of safety and retest annually.

It is indeed fortunate that heartworm is relatively easy to prevent, because treatments can be as life-threatening as the disease itself. Treatment requires a two-step process that kills the adult heartworms first and then the microfilariae. Prevention is obviously preferable; this involves a once-monthly oral or topical treatment. The most common oral preventatives include ivermectin (not suitable for some breeds), moxidectin and milbemycin oxime; the once-a-month topical drug selamectin provides heartworm protection in addition to flea, tick and other parasite control.

SCOTTISH TERRIER

When we bring home a puppy, full of the energy and exuberance that accompanies youth, we hope for a long, happy and fulfilling relationship with the new family member. Even when we adopt an older dog, we look forward to the years of companionship ahead with a new canine friend. However, aging is inevitable for all creatures, and there will come a time when our dog reaches his senior years and will need special considerations and attention to his care.

WHEN IS MY DOG A "SENIOR"?
Dogs generally are considered "seniors" at seven years of age, but that is not always accurate. A dog's senior status is better determined based on the average life expectancy for his breed, which is based on the size of the breed. Average life expectancies are considered as follows: Small breeds, 12 years or more; medium breeds, 10 years or more; large breeds, 9 years or more and giant breeds, 7 years or more. A dog is considered a senior when he has reached 75% of the average lifespan for his breed. Your Scottish Terrier has an average lifespan of 14 years,

---

SHADY PINES

Is your "golden girl" ready for the "old dogs' home"? If your dog has retained his energy and is in good shape (not overweight), you should consider yourself lucky. An active older dog who enjoys his food should not be changed to a senior food just because he is "of age." One of the super premium adult foods (or even a growth or performance brand) might be a better choice for your feisty senior citizen. Every dog's condition and needs should be evaluated by his veterinarian. The correct diet for a senior provides the appropriate caloric density to maintain the body's condition as well as balanced nutrition.

---

which is another advantage of this hardy terrier breed. Many vets contend that any age past 8 years of age is a gift, though if your dog lives to 8, he will usually last to 12 or more.

Thus, the old "seven dog years to one human year" theory is not exact. In puppyhood, a dog's year is actually comparable to more than seven human years, considering the puppy's rapid growth during his first year. Then, in adulthood, the ratio decreases. Regardless, a more viable rule of thumb is that the larger the dog, the shorter his expected lifespan. Of course, this can vary among individual dogs, with many living longer than expected, which we hope is the case!

WHAT ARE THE SIGNS OF AGING?

By the time your dog has reached his senior years, you will know him very well and, thus, the physical and behavioral changes that accompany aging should be noticeable to you. Humans and dogs share the most obvious physical sign of aging: gray hair! Graying often occurs first on the muzzle and face, around the eyes. Other telltale signs are the dogs' overall decrease in activity. Your older dog might be more content to nap and rest, and he may not show the same old enthusiasm when it's time to play in the yard or go for a walk. Other physical signs include significant weight loss or gain; more labored movement; skin and coat problems, possibly hair loss; sight and/or hearing problems; changes in toileting habits, perhaps seeming "unhousebroken" at times; tooth decay, bad breath or other mouth problems.

There are behavioral changes that go along with aging, too. There are numerous causes for behavioral changes. Sometimes a dog's apparent confusion results from a physical change like diminished sight or hearing. If his confusion causes him to be afraid, he may act aggressively or defensively. He may sleep more frequently because his daily walks, though shorter now, tire him out. He may begin to experience separation anxiety or, conversely, become less interested in petting and attention.

There also are clinical conditions that cause behavioral changes in older dogs. One such condition is known as canine cognitive dysfunction (familiarly known as "old-dog" syndrome). It can be frustrating for an owner whose dog is affected with cognitive dysfunction, as it can result in behavioral changes of all types, most seemingly unexplainable. Common changes include the

WEATHER WORRIES

Older pets are less tolerant of extremes in weather, both heat and cold. Your older dog should not spend extended periods in the sun; when outdoors in the warm weather, make sure he does not become overheated. In chilly weather, consider a sweater for your dog when outdoors and limit time spent outside. Whether or not his coat is thinning, he will need provisions to keep him warm when the weather is cold. You may even place his bed by a heating duct in your living room or bedroom.

dog's forgetting aspects of the daily routine, such as times to eat, go out for walks, relieve himself and the like. Along the same lines, you may take your dog out at the regular time for a potty trip and he may have no idea why he is there. Sometimes a placid dog will begin to show aggressive or possessive tendencies or, conversely, a hyperactive dog will start to "mellow out."

Disease also can be the cause of behavioral changes in senior dogs. Hormonal problems (Cushing's disease is common in older dogs), diabetes and thyroid disease can cause increased appetite, which can lead to aggression related to food guarding. It's better to be proactive with your senior dog, making more frequent trips to the vet if necessary and having bloodwork done to test for the diseases that can commonly befall older dogs.

This is not to say that as dogs age they all fall apart physically and become nasty in personality. The aforementioned changes are discussed to alert owners to the things that *may* happen as their dogs get older. Many hardy dogs remain active and alert well into old age. However, it can be frustrating and heartbreaking for owners to see their beloved dogs change physically and temperamentally. Just know that it's the same dog under there and that he still loves you and appreciates your care, which he needs now more than ever.

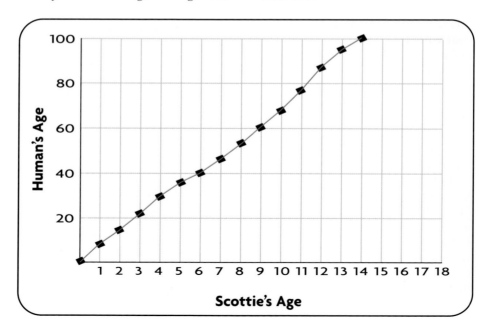

Human's Age

Scottie's Age

HOW DO I CARE FOR MY AGING DOG?

Again, every dog is an individual in terms of aging. Your dog might reach the estimated "senior" age for his breed and show no signs of slowing down. However, even if he shows no outward signs of aging, he should begin a senior-care program once he reaches the determined age. He may not show it, but he's not a pup anymore! By providing him with extra attention to his veterinary care at this age, you will be practicing good preventative medicine, ensuring that the rest of your dog's life will be as long, active, happy and healthy as possible. If you do notice indications of aging, such as graying and/or changes in sleeping, eating or toileting habits, this is a sign to set up a senior-care visit with your vet right away to make sure that these changes are not related to any health problems.

To start, senior dogs should visit the vet twice yearly for exams, routine tests and overall evaluations. Many veterinarians have special screening programs especially for senior dogs that can include a thorough physical exam; blood test to determine complete blood count; serum biochemistry test, which screens for liver, kidney and blood problems as well as cancer; urinalysis; and dental exams. With these tests, it can be determined if your dog has any health problems; the results also

CAUSES OF CHANGE

Cognitive dysfunction may not be the cause of all changes in your older dog; illness and medication can also affect him. Things like diabetes, Cushing's disease, cancer and brain tumors are serious physical problems but can cause behavioral changes as well. Older dogs are more prone to these

conditions, so they should not be overlooked as possibilities for your dog's acting not like his "old self." Any significant changes in your senior's behavior are good reasons to take your dog to the vet for a thorough exam.

Your dog's reactions to medication can cause changes as well. The various types of corticosteroids are often cited as affecting a dog's behavior. If your vet prescribes any type of drug, discuss possible side effects before administering the medication to your dog.

establish a baseline for your pet against which future test results can be compared.

In addition to these tests, your vet may suggest additional testing, including an EKG, tests for glaucoma and other problems of the eye, chest X-rays, screening for tumors, blood pressure test, test for thyroid function and screening for parasites and reassessment of his preventive program. Your vet also will ask you questions about your dog's diet and activity level, what you feed and the amounts that you feed. This information, along with his evaluation of the dog's overall condition, will enable him to suggest proper dietary changes, if needed.

This may seem like quite a work-up for your pet, but veterinarians advise that older dogs need more frequent attention so that any health problems can be detected as early as possible. Serious conditions like kidney disease, heart disease and cancer may not present outward symptoms, or the problem may go undetected if the symptoms are mistaken by owners as just part of the aging process.

There are some conditions more common in elderly dogs that are difficult to ignore. Cognitive dysfunction shares much in common with senility and Alzheimer's disease, and dogs are not immune. Dogs can become confused and/or disoriented, lose their house-training, have abnormal sleep/wake cycles and interact differently with their owners. Be heartened by the fact that, in some ways, there are more treatment options for dogs with cognitive dysfunction than for people with similar conditions. There is good evidence that continued stimulation in the form of games, play, training and exercise can help to maintain cognitive function. There are also medications (such as seligiline) and antioxidant-fortified senior diets that have been shown to be beneficial.

Cancer is also a condition more common in the elderly. Almost all of the cancers seen in people are also seen in pets. While we can't control the effects of second-hand smoke, lung cancer, which is a major killer in humans, is relatively rare in dogs. If pets are getting regular physical examinations, cancers are often detected

---

WHAT A RELIEF!
Much like young puppies, older dogs do not have as much control over their excretory functions as they do as adults. Their muscle control fades and, as such, they cannot "hold it" for as long as they used to. This is easily remedied by additional trips outside. If your dog's sight is failing, have the yard well lit at night and/or lead him to his relief site on lead. Incontinence should be discussed with your vet.

early. There are a variety of cancer therapies available today, and many pets continue to live happy lives with appropriate treatment.

Degenerative joint disease, often referred to as arthritis, is another common malady shared between elderly dogs and humans. A lifetime of wear and tear on joints, and running around at play, eventually takes it toll and results in stiffness and difficulty getting around. As dogs live longer and healthier lives, it is natural that they should eventually feel some of the effects of aging. Once again, if regular veterinary care has been available, your pet was not carrying extra pounds all those years and wearing those joints out before their time. If your pet was unfortunate enough to inherit hip dysplasia, osteochondrosis dissecans or any of the other developmental orthopedic diseases, battling the onset of degenerative joint disease was probably a longstanding goal. In any case, there are now many effective remedies for managing degenerative joint disease and a number of remarkable surgeries as well.

Aside from the extra veterinary care, there is much you can do at home to keep your older dog in good condition. The dog's diet is an important factor. If your dog's appetite decreases, he will not be getting the nutrients he needs. He also will lose weight, which is unhealthy for a dog at a proper weight. Conversely, an older dog's metabolism is slower and he usually exercises less, but he should not be allowed to become obese. Obesity in an older dog is especially risky, because extra pounds mean extra stress on the body, increasing his vulnerability to heart disease. Plus, the additional pounds make it harder for the dog to move about.

You should discuss age-related feeding changes with your vet. For a dog who has lost interest in food, it may be suggested to try some different types of food until you find something new that the dog likes. For an obese dog, a "light" formula dog food or reducing food portions may be advised, along with exercise appropriate to his physical condition and energy level.

As for exercise, despite his old age, the senior dog should not be allowed to become a "couch potato." He may not be able to handle the morning run, long walks and vigorous games of fetch, but he still needs to get up and get moving. Keep up with your daily walks, but keep the distances shorter, and let your dog set the pace. If he gets to the point where he's not up for walks, let him stroll around the yard. On the other hand, many dogs remain very active in their senior years, so base changes to the exercise program on your own individual dog and what

OUR BABY
PEPPER FRIEDMAN
1976—1984

he's capable of. Don't worry, your dog will let you know when it's time to rest.

Keep up with your grooming routine as you always have. Be extra diligent about checking the skin and coat for problems. Older dogs can experience thinning coats as a normal aging process, but they can also lose hair as a result of medical problems. Some thinning is normal, but patches of baldness or the loss of significant amounts of hair is not.

Hopefully, you've been regular with brushing your dog's teeth throughout his life. Healthy teeth directly affect overall good health. We already know that bacteria from gum infections can enter the dog's body through the damaged gums and travel to the organs. At a stage in life when his organs don't function as well as they used to, you don't want anything to put additional strain on them. Clean teeth also contribute to a healthy immune system. Offering the

dental-type chews in addition to toothbrushing can help, as these remove plaque and tartar as the dog chews.

Along with the same good care you've given him all of his life, pay a little extra attention to your dog in his senior years and keep up with twice-yearly trips to the vet. The sooner a problem is uncovered, the greater the chances of a full recovery.

SAYING GOODBYE
While you can help your dog live as long a life as possible, you can't help him live forever. A dog's lifespan is short when compared to that of a human, so it is inevitable that pet owners will experience loss. To many, losing a beloved dog is like losing a family member. Our dogs are part of our lives every day, are our true loyal friends and always seem to know when it's time to comfort us, to celebrate with us or to just provide the company of a caring friend. Even if we know that our dog is nearing his final days, we can never quite prepare for his being gone.

Many dogs live out long lives and simply die of old age. Others unfortunately are taken suddenly by illness or accident, and still others find their senior years compromised by disease and physical problems. In some of these cases, owners find themselves having to make difficult decisions.

SHOWING YOUR
SCOTTISH TERRIER

Is dog showing in your blood? Are you excited by the idea of gaiting your handsome Scottish Terrier around the ring to the thunderous applause of an enthusiastic audience? Are you certain that your beloved Scottish Terrier is flawless? You are not alone! Every loving owner thinks that his dog has no faults, or too few to mention. No matter how many times an owner reads over the breed standard, he cannot find any faults in his aristocratic companion dog. If this sounds like you, and if you are considering entering your Scottish Terrier in a dog show, here are some basic questions to ask yourself:

- Did you purchase a "show-quality" puppy from the breeder?
- Is your puppy at least six months of age?
- Does the puppy exhibit correct show type for his breed?
- Does your puppy have any disqualifying faults?
- Is your Scottish Terrier registered with the American Kennel Club?
- How much time do you have to devote to training, grooming, conditioning and exhibiting your Scottish Terrier?

- Do you understand the rules and regulations of a dog show?
- Do you have time to learn how to show your dog properly?
- Do you have the financial resources to invest in showing your dog?
- Will you show the dog yourself or hire a professional handler?
- Do you have a vehicle that can accommodate your weekend trips to the dog shows?

Success in the show ring requires more than a pretty face, a waggy tail and a pocketful of liver. Even though dog shows can be exciting and enjoyable, the sport of conformation makes great demands on the exhibitors and the dogs. Winning exhibitors live for their dogs, devoting time and money to their dogs' presentation, conditioning and training. Very few novices, even those with good dogs, will find themselves in the winners' circle, though it does happen. Don't be disheartened, though. Every exhibitor began as a novice and worked his way up to the Group ring. It's the "working your way up" part that you must keep in mind.

Assuming that you have purchased a puppy of the correct type and quality for showing, let's begin to examine the world of showing and what's required to get started. Although the entry fee into a dog show is nominal, there are lots of other hidden costs involved with "finishing" your Scottish Terrier, that is, making him a champion. Things like equipment, travel, training and conditioning all cost money. A more serious campaign will

include fees for a professional handler, boarding, cross-country travel and advertising. Top-winning show dogs represent an investment of over $100,000 per year. Keep in mind that few dog shows offer cash prizes! For the 100,000 reasons listed above, many dog owners are opting to participate in United Kennel Club shows, where professional handlers are not permitted. These shows are more owner-oriented and, for many, more rewarding than AKC events.

Many owners, on the other hand, enter their "average" Scottish Terriers in dog shows for the fun and enjoyment of it. Dog showing makes an absorbing hobby with many rewards for dogs and owners alike. If you're having fun, meeting other people who share your interests and enjoying the overall experience, you likely will catch the "bug." Once the dog-show bug bites, its effects can last a lifetime; it's like a deer tick, but good instead. Soon you will be envisioning yourself in the center ring at the Westminster Kennel Club Dog Show in New York City, competing for the prestigious Best in Show cup. This magical dog show is televised annually from Madison Square Garden, and the victorious dog becomes a celebrity overnight. Over a half dozen Scotties have pulled off this feat!

DRESS THE PART

It's a dog show, so don't forget your costume. Even though the show is about the dog, you also must play your role well. You have been cast as the "dog handler" and you must smartly dress the part. Solid colors make a nice complement to the dog's coat, and choose colors that contrast. You don't want to be wearing white if you have a white dog, or brown if you have a brown dog. Whether the show is indoors or out, you still must dress properly. You want the judge to perceive you as professional, so polish, polish, polish! And don't forget to wear sensible shoes; remember, you have to gait around the ring with your dog.

AKC CONFORMATION SHOWING

GETTING STARTED

Visiting a dog show as a spectator is a great place to start. Pick up the show catalog to find out what time your breed is being shown, who is judging the breed and in which ring the classes will be held. To start, Scottish Terriers compete against other Scottish Terriers, and the winner is selected as Best of Breed by the judge. This is the procedure for each breed. At a Group show, all of the Best of Breed winners go on to compete for Group One in their respective group. For example, all Best of Breed winners for each breed in the Terrier Group compete against each other; this is done for all seven groups. Finally, all seven group winners go head to head in the ring for the Best in Show award.

What most spectators don't understand is the basic idea of conformation. A dog show is often referred to as a "conformation" show. This means that the judge should decide how each dog stacks up (conforms) to the breed standard for his given breed: how well does this Scottish Terrier conform to the ideal representative detailed in the standard? Ideally, this is what happens. In reality, however, this ideal often gets slighted as the

One last time around the ring to determine a winner!

judge compares Scottish Terrier #1 to Scottish Terrier #2. Again, the ideal is that each dog is judged based on his merits in comparison to his breed standard, not in comparison to the other dogs in the ring. It is easier for judges to compare dogs of the same breed to decide which they think is the better specimen; in the Group and Best in Show ring, however, it is very difficult to compare one breed to another, like apples to oranges. Thus the dog's conformation to the breed standard (not to mention good handling and advertising dollars) is essential to his success.

The breed standard, which is drafted and approved by the breed's national parent club, the Scottish Terrier Club of America, is then submitted to the American Kennel Club (AKC). The dog described in the standard is the perfect dog of that breed, and breeders keep their eye on the standard when they choose which dogs to breed, hoping to get closer and closer to the ideal with each litter.

Another good first step for the novice is to join a dog club. You will be astonished by the many and different kinds of dog clubs in the country, with about 5,000 clubs holding events every year. Most clubs require that prospective new members present two letters of recommendation from existing members. Perhaps you've made some friends visiting a show held by a particular club and you would like to join that club. Dog clubs may specialize in a single breed, like a local or regional Scottish Terrier club, or in a specific pursuit, such as obedience, tracking or hunting tests. There are all-breed clubs for all dog enthusiasts, which sponsor special training days, seminars on topics like grooming or handling or lectures on breeding or canine

genetics. There are also clubs that specialize in certain types of dogs, like herding dogs, hunting dogs, companion dogs, etc.

A parent club is the national organization, sanctioned by the American Kennel Club, which promotes and safeguards its breed in the country. The Scottish Terrier Club of America was formed in 1900 and can be reached via the Internet at http://clubs.akc.org/stca/. The parent club holds an annual national specialty show, usually in a different city each year, in which many of the country's top dogs, handlers and breeders gather to compete. At a specialty show, only members of a single breed are invited to participate. There are also Group specialties, in which all members of a Group are invited. For more information about dog clubs in your area, contact the AKC at www.akc.org on the Internet or write them at their Raleigh, NC address.

HOW SHOWS ARE ORGANIZED
Three kinds of conformation show are offered by the AKC. There is the all-breed show, in which all AKC-recognized breeds can compete; the specialty show, which is for one breed only and usually sponsored by the breed's parent club, and the Group show, for all breeds in one of the seven AKC groups. The Scottish Terrier competes in the Terrier Group.

You need a great Scottie, an experienced Scottie groomer and an experienced Scottie handler to show the judge that you deserve the ticket!

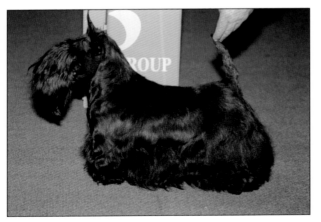

As the judge completes his evaluation, he may be most concerned about the dogs' gait. That a dog can move well indicates to the judge that it is soundly and properly constructed.

For a dog to become an AKC champion of record, the dog must earn 15 points at shows. The points must be awarded by at least three different judges and must include two "majors" under different judges. A "major" is a three-, four- or five-point win, and the number of points per win is determined by the number of dogs competing in the show on that day. Dogs that are absent or are excused are not counted. The number of points that are awarded varies from breed to breed. More dogs are needed to attain a major in more popular breeds, and fewer dogs are needed in less popular breeds. Yearly, the AKC evaluates the number of dogs in competition in each division (there are 14 divisions in all, based on geography) and may or may not change the numbers of dogs required for each number of points. For example, a major in Division 2 (Delaware, New Jersey and Pennsylvania) recently

SHOW POTENTIAL

How possible is it to predict how your ten-week-old puppy will eventually do in the show ring? Most show dogs reach their prime at around three years of age, when their bodies are physically mature and their coats are in "full bloom." Experienced breeders, having watched countless pups grow into Best of Breed winners, recognize the glowing attributes that spell "show potential." When selecting a puppy for show, it's best to trust the breeder to recommend which puppy will best suit your aspirations. Some breeders recommend starting with a male puppy that is likely more "typey" than his female counterpart.

FOR MORE INFORMATION....
For reliable, up-to-date information about registration, dog shows and other canine competitions, contact one of the national registries by mail or via the Internet.

American Kennel Club
5580 Centerview Dr., Raleigh, NC 27606-3390
www.akc.org

United Kennel Club
100 E. Kilgore Road, Kalamazoo, MI 49002
www.ukcdogs.com

Canadian Kennel Club
89 Skyway Ave., Suite 100, Etobicoke, Ontario M9W 6R4 Canada
www.ckc.ca

The Kennel Club
1-5 Clarges St., Piccadilly, London W1Y 8AB, UK
www.the-kennel-club.org.uk

required 17 dogs or 16 bitches for a three-point major, 29 dogs or 27 bitches for a four-point major and 51 dogs or 46 bitches for a five-point major. The Scottish Terrier usually attracts impressive numbers at all-breed shows, though not as many as breeds like the Poodle or Labrador Retriever.

Only one dog and one bitch of each breed can win points at a given show. There are no "co-ed" classes except for champions of record. Dogs and bitches do not compete against each other until they are champions. Dogs that are not champions (referred to as "class dogs") compete in one of five classes. The class in which a dog is entered depends on age and previous show wins. First, there is the Puppy Class (sometimes divided further into classes for 6- to 9-month-olds and 9- to 12-month-olds); next is the Novice Class (for dogs that have no points toward their championship and whose only first-place wins have come in the Puppy Class or the Novice Class, the latter class limited to three first places); then there is the American-bred Class (for dogs bred in the US); the Bred-by-Exhibitor Class (for dogs handled by their breeders or by immediate family members of their breeders) and the Open Class (for any non-champions). Any dog may enter the Open class, regardless of age or win history, but, to be competitive, the dog should be older and have ring experience.

The judge at the show begins judging the dogs in the Puppy Class(es) and proceeds through the other classes. The judge awards first through fourth place in each class. The first-place winners of each class then compete with one another in the Winners Class to determine Winners Dog. The judge then starts over with the bitches, beginning with the Puppy Class(es) and proceeding up to the Winners Class to award Winners Bitch, just as he did with the dogs. A Reserve Winners Dog and Reserve Winners Bitch are also selected; these could be awarded the points in the case of a disqualification.

The Winners Dog and Winners Bitch are the two that are awarded the points for their breed. They then go on to compete with any champions of record (often called "specials") of their breed that are entered in the show. The champions may be dogs or bitches; in this class, all are shown together. The judge reviews the Winners Dog and Winners Bitch along with all of the champions to select the Best of Breed winner. The Best of Winners is selected between the Winners Dog and Winners Bitch; if one of these two is selected Best of Breed as well, he or she is automatically determined Best of Winners. Lastly, the judge selects Best of Opposite Sex to the Best of Breed winner. The Best of Breed winner then goes on to the Group competition.

At a Group or all-breed show, the Best of Breed winners from each breed are divided into their respective groups to compete against one another for Group One through Group Four. Group One (first place) is awarded to the dog that best lives up to the ideal for his breed as described in the standard. A Group judge, therefore, must have a thorough working knowledge of many breed standards. After placements have been made in each Group,

ON THE MOVE
The truest test of a dog's proper structure is his gait, how well the dog moves. The American Kennel Club defines gait as "the pattern of footsteps at various rates of speed, each pattern distinguished by a particular rhythm and footfall." That the dog moves smoothly and effortlessly indicates to the judge that the dog's structure is well made. From the four-beat gallop, the fastest of canine gaits, to the high-lifting hackney gait, each breed varies in its correct gait; breeds are not all expected to move in the same way. Each breed standard defines the correct gait for that breed and often identifies movement faults, such as toeing in, side-winding, over-reaching and crossing over.

the seven Group One winners (from the Terrier Group, Toy Group, Hound Group, etc.) compete against each other for the top honor, Best in Show.

There are different ways to find out about dog shows in your area. The American Kennel Club's monthly magazine, the *American Kennel Gazette* is accompanied by the *Events Calendar*; this magazine is available through subscription. You can also look on the AKC's and your parent club's websites for information, and check the event listings in your local newspaper.

Your Scottish Terrier must be six months of age or older and registered with the AKC in order to be entered in AKC-sanctioned shows in which there are classes for the Scottish Terrier. Your Scottish Terrier also must not possess any disqualifying faults and must be sexually intact. The reason for the latter is simple: dog shows are the proving grounds to determine which dogs and bitches are worthy of being bred. If they cannot be bred, that defeats the purpose! On that note, only dogs that have achieved championships, thus proving their excellent quality, should be bred. If you have spayed or neutered your dog, however, there are many AKC events other than conformation, such as obedience trials, agility trials and the Canine Good Citizen program, in which you and your Scottish Terrier can participate.

OTHER TYPES OF COMPETITION

OBEDIENCE TRIALS

Mrs. Helen Whitehouse Walker, a Standard Poodle fancier, can be credited with introducing obedience trials to the United States. In the 1930s, she designed a series of exercises based on those of the Associated Sheep, Police, Army Dog Society of Great Britain. These exercises were intended to evaluate the working relationship between dog and owner. Since those early days of the sport in the US, obedience trials have grown more and more popular, and now more than 2,000 trials each year attract over 100,000 dogs and their owners. Any dog registered with the AKC, regardless of neutering or other disqualifications that would preclude his entry in conformation competition, can participate in obedience.

There are three levels of difficulty in obedience competition. The first (and easiest) level is the Novice, in which dogs can earn the Companion Dog (CD) title. The intermediate level is the Open level, in which the Companion Dog Excellent (CDX) title is awarded. The advanced level is the Utility level, in which dogs compete for the Utility Dog (UD) title. Classes at each level are further divided into "A" and "B," with "A" for beginners and "B" for those with more experience. In order to win a title at a given level, a dog must earn three "legs." A "leg" is accomplished when a dog scores 170 or higher (200 is a perfect score). The scoring system gets a little trickier, because a dog must score more than 50% of the points available for each exercise in order to actually earn the points. Available points for each exercise range between 20 and 40.

A dog must complete different exercises at each level of obedience. The Novice exercises are the easiest, with the Open and finally the Utility levels progressing in difficulty. Examples of Novice exercises are on- and off-lead heeling, a figure-8 pattern, performing a recall (or come), long sit and long down and standing for examination. In the Open level, the Novice-level exercises are required again, but this time without a leash and for longer durations. In addition, the dog must clear a broad jump, retrieve over a jump and drop on recall. In the Utility level, the exercises are quite difficult, including executing basic commands based on hand signals, following a complex heeling pattern, locating articles based on scent discrimination and completing jumps at the handler's direction.

Once he's earned the UD title, a dog can go on to win the prestigious title of Utility Dog Excellent (UDX) by winning "legs" in ten shows. Additionally, Utility Dogs who win "legs" in Open B and Utility B earn points toward the lofty title of Obedience Trial Champion (OTCh.). Established in 1977 by the AKC, this title requires a dog to earn 100 points as well as three first places in a combination of Open B and Utility B classes under three

different judges. The "brass ring" of obedience competition is the AKC's National Obedience Invitational. This is an exclusive competition for only the cream of the obedience crop. In order to qualify for the invitational, a dog must be either ranked in the top 25 all-breeds in obedience or be ranked in the top three for his breed in obedience. The title at stake here is that of National Obedience Champion (NOC).

AGILITY TRIALS

Agility trials became sanctioned by the AKC in August 1994, when the first licensed agility trials were held. Since that time, agility certainly has grown in popularity by leaps and bounds, literally! The AKC allows all registered breeds (including Miscellaneous Class breeds) to participate, providing the dog is 12 months of age or older. Agility is designed so that the handler demonstrates how well the dog can work at his side. The handler directs his dog through, over, under and around an obstacle course that includes jumps, tires, the dog walk, weave poles, pipe tunnels, collapsed tunnels and more. While working his way through the course, the dog must keep one eye and ear on the handler and the rest of his body on the course. The handler runs along with the dog, giving verbal and hand signals to guide the dog through the course.

The first organization to promote agility trials in the US was the United States Dog Agility Association, Inc. (USDAA). Established in 1986, the USDAA sparked the formation of many member clubs around the country. To participate in USDAA trials, dogs must be at least 18 months of age.

The USDAA and AKC both offer titles to winning dogs, although the exercises and requirements of the two organizations differ. Agility Dog (AD), Advanced Agility Dog (AAD) and Master Agility Dog (MAD) are the titles offered by the USDAA, while the AKC offers Novice Agility (NA), Open Agility (OA), Agility Excellent (AX) and Master Agility Excellent (MX). Beyond these four AKC titles, dogs can win additional titles in "jumper" classes: Jumper with Weave Novice (NAJ), Open (OAJ) and Excellent (MXJ). The ultimate title in AKC agility is MACH, Master Agility Champion. Dogs can continue to add number designations to the MACH title, indicating how many times the dog has met the title's requirements (MACH1, MACH2 and so on).

Agility trials are a great way to keep your dog active, and they will keep you running, too! You should join a local agility club to learn more about the sport. These clubs offer sessions in which you can introduce your dog to the various obstacles as well as training classes to prepare him for competition. In no time, your dog will be climbing A-frames, crossing the dog walk and flying over hurdles, all with you right beside him. Your heart will leap every time your dog jumps through the hoop—and you'll be having just as much (if not more) fun!

TRACKING

Tracking tests are exciting ways to test your Scottish Terrier's instinctive scenting ability on a competitive level. All dogs have a nose, and all breeds are welcome in tracking tests. The first AKC-licensed tracking test took place in 1937 as part of the Utility level at an obedience trial, and thus competitive tracking was officially begun. The first title, Tracking Dog (TD), was offered in 1947, ten years after the first official tracking test. It was not until 1980 that the AKC added the title Tracking Dog Excellent (TDX), which was followed by the title Versatile Surface Tracking (VST) in 1995. Champion Tracker (CT) is awarded to a dog who has earned all three of these titles.

The TD level is the first and most basic level in tracking, progressing in difficulty to the TDX and then the VST. A dog must follow a track laid by a human 30 to 120 minutes prior in order to earn the TD title. The track is about 500 yards long and contains up to 5 directional changes. At the next level, the TDX, the dog must follow a 3- to 5-hour-old track over a course that is up to 1,000 yards long and has up to 7 directional changes. In the most difficult level, the VST, the track is up to 5 hours old and located in an urban setting.

EARTHDOG EVENTS

Earthdog trials are held for those breeds that were developed to "go to ground." These dogs were bred to go down into badger and fox holes and bring out the quarry. Breeds such as Parson Russelll Terriers, Dachshunds and other short-legged hunters are used in this fashion. Earthdog trials test the dog in a simulated hunting situation in which trenches are dug and lined usually with wood. The scent of the rat is laid in the trench, and the quarry is a caged rat at the end of the tunnel. The dog can see and smell the rat but cannot touch or harm the quarry in any way.

There are four levels in earthdog trials. The first, Introduction to Quarry, is for beginners and uses a 10-foot tunnel. No title is awarded at this level. The Junior Earthdog (JE) title is awarded at the next level, which uses a 30-foot tunnel with 3 90-degree turns. Two qualifying JE runs are required for a dog to earn the title. The next level, Senior Earthdog (SE), uses the same length tunnel and number of turns as in the JE level but also has a false den and exit and requires the dog to come out of the tunnel when called. To try for the SE title, a dog must have at least his JE; the SE title requires three qualifying runs at this level. The most difficult of the earthdog tests, Master Earthdog (ME), again uses the 30-foot tunnel with three 90-degree turns, with a false entrance, exit and den. The dog is required to enter in the right place and, in this test, honor another working dog. The ME title requires four qualifying runs, and a dog must have earned his SE title to attempt the ME level.

This Scottie is getting a thorough pre-show grooming to look his best for the judge in the ring.

INDEX

My Scottish Terrier

PUT YOUR PUPPY'S FIRST PICTURE HERE

Dog's Name _____

Date _____ Photographer _____